Autobiography and National Identity in the Americas

Communities are to be distinguished, not by their falsity/genuineness, but by the style in which they are imagined.

Benedict Anderson

Telling the truth about the self, constituting the self as complete subject—it is a fantasy. In spite of the fact that autobiography is impossible, this in no way prevents it from existing.

Philippe Lejeune

Autobiography and National Identity in the Americas

Steven V. Hunsaker

New World Studies

A. James Arnold, editor

University Press of Virginia

Charlottesville & London

The University Press of Virginia
Printed in the United States of America

First published 1999

∞ The paper used in this publication meets the minimum requirements of the
American National Standard for Information Sciences—Permanence of Paper for
Printed Library Materials, ANSI Z39.48-1984.

Library of Congress Cataloging-in-Publication Data

Hunsaker, Steven V., 1965–
    Autobiography and national identity in the Americas / Steven V. Hunsaker.
        p.   cm.—(New World studies)
    Includes bibliographical references and index.
    ISBN 0-8139-1844-8 (alk. paper). — ISBN 0-8139-1845-6 (paper : alk. paper)
    1. Minorities—America—Biography—History and criticism. 2. Autobiogra-
phy—History and criticism. 3. National characteristics, American. 4. Nationalism—America—History—20th century. 5. Ethnicity—America—History—20th
century. 6. America—Ethnic relations.
I. Title. II. Series.
E29.A1H86 1999
305.8—dc21   98-42102
                                                                CIP

For Susan

Contents

Acknowledgments

My thanks to my wife, Susan, and to our children, Allison, Camille, and Grant. Susan's help has been indispensable as I have thought through various issues; her comments have reduced pretense and increased insight. Although I am listed as the sole author of this book, there would be no book without her patient encouragement, listening ear, and steady interest in the project. Thank you.

Special thanks to Earl Fitz, a pioneer in the study of inter-American literature and a mentor whose example as both scholar and family man continues to inspire me. Thanks as well to Tom Beebee, whose wit and intellect have sharpened my work.

A sincere thank-you to the two anonymous readers of the manuscript, whose careful reading and insightful commentary strengthened this project significantly.

Finally, many thanks to Cathie Brettschneider and the staff at the University Press of Virginia for their professionalism and support.

An earlier version of chapter 3 appeared in the *Canadian Review of Studies in Nationalism*. Likewise, an earlier version of chapter 4 appeared in *Biography: An Interdisciplinary Quarterly* 20.4 (fall 1997), © Copyright 1997 by the Biographical Research Center.

A Note on Translation

Translations from Spanish texts and criticism in Portuguese are always mine. In chapter 2 I cite *Child of the Dark*, an English translation of Carolina Maria de Jesus's Portuguese narrative, but when that version seems inadequate I supply my own translation. In chapter 3 I cite *White Niggers of America*, the English translation of Pierre Vallières's autobiography, but translations from works of criticism in French in chapter 3 are mine.

Abbreviations

DO   *Days of Obligation: An Argument with My Mexican Father* (Richard Rodriguez)

HB   *Halfbreed* (Maria Campbell)

IC   *Imagined Communities: Reflections on the Origin and Spread of Nationalism* (Benedict Anderson)

LMEAM   *La montaña es algo más que una inmensa estepa verde* (Omar Cabezas)

MLRM   *Me llamo Rigoberta Menchú y así me nació la conciencia* (Elizabeth Burgos, ed.)

QD   *Quarto de despejo: Diário de uma favelada* (Carolina Maria de Jesus)

RAGB   *Rites: A Guatemalan Boyhood* (Victor Perera)

SMPH   *"Si me permiten hablar . . .": Testimonio de Domitila, una mujer de las minas de Bolivia* (Moema Viezzer, ed.)

WN   *White Niggers of America: The Precocious Autobiography of a Quebec "Terrorist"* (Pierre Vallières)

WW   *The Woman Warrior: Memoirs of a Girlhood among Ghosts* (Maxine Hong Kingston)

Autobiography and National
Identity in the Americas

Introduction: National Identity and the Autobiographical Self

The authors of the texts considered in the following chapters ask what amounts to the same question in different national settings. From Guatemala to English Canada, Brazil, and Bolivia, to Nicaragua and French Canada, to Guatemala again and then to the United States, that question is: Who am I, and what role does nation play in shaping my identity? Although the question remains largely the same from one text to another, the use of nation as a source of identity differs radically with ethnicity, gender, and economic situation.

This uneven pattern supports Benedict Anderson's contention that the nation becomes meaningful when it is imagined as a limited, sovereign community. This is not, however, to say that nations spring into existence when we learn to think of ourselves in terms of shared language, traditions, and territory. The fact, as Anthony D. Smith observes, that "modern nations have been built on the foundations of pre-existing ethnies" and that "many ethnic nationalisms can draw on ethnic sentiments and shared memories, myths, symbols and values" ("Culture," 446) means that the particular cultural shape that a nation assumes will always be in large measure predetermined for the individual contemplating his or her place in it. However, the individual's sense of *national identity*, as opposed to the form of the nation per se, draws on the historical background that Smith describes in a much less restrictive fashion. This background constitutes what Ulf Hannerz calls the "tools of identity and imagination," which are "not always . . . equally available to all nation builders, nor are the contexts of assembling, disassembling or reconstructing all the same" ("Withering Away," 389). The nation predates the individual, but as the narratives considered here show, the meaning and the value of that community for the individual are subject to question, challenge, and nearly constant revision.

There are myriad academic definitions of "nation," but the importance of territory, history, and some shared means of self-definition (whether linguistic, religious, or ancestral) are common to all. For example, Anthony D. Smith, perhaps the most prolific contemporary theorist of the nation, suggests the following traits as characteristic of the "ideal type" of the nation.

1. the growth of myths and memories of common ancestry and history of the cultural unit of population;
2. the formation of a shared public culture based on an indigenous resource (language, religion, etc.);
3. the delimitation of a compact historic territory, or homeland;
4. the unification of local economic units into a single socio-economic unit based on the single culture and homeland;
5. the growth of common codes and institutions of a single legal order, with common rights and duties for all members. ("Problem," 381)

It is important to note that Smith uses language that merges nation and state, especially in the emphasis on legal and economic structure in points 4 and 5. Walker Connor, another prominent theorist of ethnic and national identity, offers the polar opposite of Smith's definition, discussing nation in terms of myth, memory, and common ancestry with no reference to the legal and economic organization that is so important in Smith's "ideal type." "In its pristine meaning," Connor says, "a nation is a group of people whose members believe that they are ancestrally related. It is the largest group to share such a myth of common descent; it is, in a sentient sense, the fully extended family. In some cases, the myth of common descent has been given specific content through putative ties to a legendary figure (Noah has been particularly popular) or to an earlier people (Trojans, Phoenecians, and one of the ten lost tribes of Israel have all been broadly claimed as progenitors)" ("Nation and Myth," 48). If Smith's definition suggests a legal character that makes the nation resemble too closely the state, Connor's definition is perhaps too loose, defining the nation in ways that apply equally well to ethnic groups. Nonetheless, it is no easy thing to separate these terms, as evident in the overlap when Smith says:

> I define an ethnic community (or "ethnie") as a named human popu-
> lation of alleged common ancestry, shared memories and elements
> of common culture with a link to a specific territory and a measure
> of solidarity; a "nation" as a named human population sharing a his-
> toric territory, common myths and historical memories, a mass, public
> culture, a common economy and common legal rights and duties;
> and "nationalism" as an ideological movement for the attainment
> and maintenance of autonomy, unity and identity on behalf of a
> population some of whose members deem themselves to constitute
> an actual or potential "nation." ("Culture," 447)

Smith argues elsewhere that the nation is "a subcategory of, and devel-opment out of, the far more common phenomenon of ethnic community" ("Problem," 382), suggesting that the differences between nation and eth-nic community are differences of degree and not differences of kind.

Recognizing the close ties between the ethnic group and the nation, I choose "nation" rather than "ethnicity" as the central defining term of this study. "Nation" strikes me as the more appropriate term because even when they portray themselves specifically as members of minority ethnic groups, the autobiographers whom I consider in this study discuss large-scale group identity in terms of resisting the reach of an aggressive nation that encompasses several ethnicities or, on the other hand, in terms of forming, joining, or modifying such an inclusive nation. In brief, because Anderson describes what is ultimately national identity rather than the na-tion itself, his model is more useful for my purposes than the more nor-mative and sociologically oriented work of other theorists. To take the prime example, in a passage that informs much of the discussion that fol-lows, Anderson says of the nation, the "imagined community": "It is *imagined* because the members of even the smallest nation will never know most of their fellow-members, meet them, or even hear of them, yet in the minds of each lives the image of their communion" (*IC*, 6).

Departing dramatically from theories of national identity based in blood, Anderson argues that nationality depends less on race or the place of our birth than on the ability to imagine oneself as part of a national community. Anderson's subjective terms allow for a great deal of flexibil-ity in the definition of nations, but they also expose him to Smith's charge that "since any community above the level of the face-to-face is imagined, this kind of definition is more suggestive than helpful" ("Problem," 380). Yet, I find Anderson helpful because his emphasis on the subjective nature of national identity coincides with my interest in the subjective and strategic nature of national identity in autobiographical writing. Autobiographers write the story of identity with a reader in mind. Similarly, the way autobiographers imagine their national community depends on the anticipated audience. To summarize, Anderson is right to describe national identity in terms of imagination, but not in the unifying and inclusive way he intends. Although national identity is an act of imagination, there is no guarantee that a group of potential compatriots will imagine the community uniformly—or even care to imagine it at all. Speaking of the impossibility of defining the national "will," Smith argues, "apart from a daily plebiscite, there is no means of ascertaining its nature, or deciding whether it was in fact a true and free expression of the 'will of the people,' or of the individuals who compose the nation. There is also the problem of deciding who shall count as 'the people.' It has been all too easy for demagogues to feel that they alone can interpret the popular will and decide who the people are" (*Nations and Nationalism*, 148). Widely disparate definitions of "the people" appear even in ethnically homogenous situations, and they are only compounded in the multiethnic "nations" discussed here. That strain between hegemonic and resistant forms of national identity makes the multiple forms and modes of national identity a key element of this study.

The tension between the compelled membership of diverse cultural groups in one hegemonic "nation" and the resistance of such moves through ethnically based nationalism have made Chechnya, Kosovo, and Bosnia-Herzegovina household words, and it is central to my discussion of *Me llamo Rigoberta Menchú* in chapter 1. I move, chapter by chapter, from that starting point to narratives that stress the opposite concern: a desire to pull away from ethnic differentiation toward a broad-based cultural nationalism.

My debt to Anderson's notion of the "imagined community" is clear, but I am more interested in ways that the authors whom I read require modification of Anderson's take on nations and national identity than in ways that they validate his ideas. In other words, this book is not an attempt to demonstrate theoretical "fit" with Anderson from text to text or from nation to nation. I take issue with Anderson's optimistic portrayal of national identity, finding evidence in every text I consider that the "imagined community" is more idiosyncratic, complex, and divisive than Anderson acknowledges.

Autobiographers from Guatemala, Canada, Brazil, Bolivia, Quebec, Nicaragua, and the United States imagine new versions of the community against dominant forms of national identity in an attempt to clear space for themselves within otherwise restrictive national situations. In every case, portraying oneself as a nationalist is not a matter of assuming a predetermined political stance but of speaking against previous models of national identity to establish new, more liberating, or more convenient models of nationality. That sense of national identity is most frequently developed through syncretic strategies that lead to a plural sense of self. The effort to imagine the nation anew and to thereby choose and fashion identity through the combination of disparate and often contradictory elements is common to all nine texts. These texts claim implicitly the power that Julia Kristeva claims explicitly: the right and the power to identify oneself by selecting, discarding, altering, and preserving models of religious, gender, political, ethnic, and national identity. Kristeva states:

> the fact of belonging to a set is a matter of choice. Beyond the *origins* that have assigned to us biological identity papers and a linguistic, religious, social, political, historical place, the freedom of contemporary individuals may be argued according to their ability to *choose* their membership, while the democratic capability of a nation and social group is revealed by the right it affords individuals to exercise that choice. Thus when I say that I have chosen cosmopolitanism, this means that I have, against origins and starting from them, chosen a transnational or international position situated at the crossing of boundaries. (*Nations without Nationalism*, 15–16)

The autobiographers whom I study here seem to take that power to choose for granted, but the assumption notwithstanding, they must confront the unchosen elements of identity that Anthony Smith summarizes as "shared memories, myths, symbols and values" ("Culture," 446), which determine nationality both in common parlance and in the legal sense. Since preexisting models and patterns weigh heavily, nationality for these autobiographers is never simply a matter of deciding to be or to do something new. The conflict between chosen and unchosen patterns of national identity is just one of the forms that the controversy over national identities takes.

For these autobiographers and for us as their readers, reliance on "inevitable" forms of national identity leads to an understanding of the nation as an entity independent of—and thus imposed on—those who compose it rather than as their creation. Consequently, national identity has value as a "natural" quality, and patriotism becomes an ideal beyond challenge.

Of the ways that the ideological edge of patriotism and national identity becomes invisible, Anderson states:

> Something of the nature of this political love can be deciphered from the ways in which language describes its object: either in the vocabulary of kinship (motherland, *Vaterland, patria*) or that of home (*Heimat* or *tanah air* [earth and water, the phrase for the Indonesian's native archipelago]). Both idioms denote something to which one is naturally tied. As we have seen earlier, in everything 'natural' there is always something unchosen. In this way, nation-ness is assimilated to skin-colour, gender, parentage, and birth-era—all those things one can not help. And in these 'natural ties' one senses what one might call the 'beauty of *gemeinschaft*'. To put it another way, precisely because such ties are not chosen, they have about them a halo of disinterestedness. (*IC*, 143)

Anderson gives special importance to those elements of national identity that cannot be chosen. There is, however, a great deal more to be said about the ideological formation of the groups to which we are "naturally tied," if only because these nine narratives indicate that at all points in a wide range of political and economic circumstances the individual autobiographer *chooses* the form that his or her national identity takes. I hasten to add that I am not suggesting that the individual enjoys absolute freedom to determine identity vis-à-vis the nation, but that within the more or less restrictive conditions that they confront, the authors of these narratives *portray* themselves selecting, rejecting, shaping, and reimagining the nation to suit their own political and ideological goals. As K. Anthony Appiah commonsensically notes, "we make up selves from a tool kit of options made available by our culture and society. We do make choices, but we do not determine the options among which we choose" ("Identity," 155). This study is an effort to expand and refine Anderson's thesis by examining how and why individuals choose to imagine their communities in new ways and then identify themselves through autobiographical writing.

   I use the term "autobiographical writing" rather than "autobiography" because I include forms as diverse as the personal essay, the testimonial narrative, and the diary within that general rubric. Rather than indicating ignorance of traditional definitions of autobiography, the formal range of these texts signals my effort to include a broad variety of responses to the nation through various kinds and forms of personal writing. I am aware, for example, that Philippe Lejeune excludes many of the texts that I discuss when he defines autobiography as "retrospective prose narrative written by a real person concerning his own existence, where the focus is his individual life, in particular the story of his personality" (*On Autobiography*, 4). Although the narratives of Richard Rodriguez and Carolina Maria de Jesus are not strictly retrospective in the way Lejeune uses the word, and despite the fact that Domitila Barrios de Chungara is not interested in telling the story of her personality, the most serious difference between Lejeune's definition and the narratives that I discuss here lies in his insistence that the focus of autobiography is the individual life. I am also aware that the critical tradition that has grown up around *testimonio* has long insisted on an essential difference between autobiography and that more group-oriented form. Recognizing arguments by John Beverley, to take just one example, that *testimonio* is "not so much concerned with the life of a 'problematic hero' . . . as with a problematic collective social situation that the narrator lives with or alongside others" ("All Things," 15), I maintain that whereas *testimonio*, personal essays, and journals are not autobiography in the strict sense, all three forms are certainly *autobiographical*. George Yúdice makes essentially this very argument when he states, "testimonial writing, as the word indicates, promotes expression of personal experience. That personal experience, of course, is the *collective* struggle against oppression from oligarchy, military, and transnational capital" ("*Testimonio* and Postmodernism," 54). Whatever the ideological forces that shape the understanding and presentation of a life, it is the narration of the life of the self—whether in isolation or in relation—that forms the essential heart of these narratives.

I find that most of the autobiographers in this study, rather than opposing the identity of the isolated individual or the "self-made man" to a communal identity, identify themselves through groups in ways that challenge traditional forms of autobiographical identity. Although this is not true in every case, the female autobiographers tend to defy traditional gender roles as well as restrictive forms of national and personal identity in their narratives. Most famously, Rigoberta Menchú insists that her narrative is the history of a people rather than the story of an individual life. Similarly, Domitila Barrios de Chungara shifts the ideological focus of her narrative to the community as part of her effort to redefine the nation in liberating rather than oppressive ways. Maxine Hong Kingston, on the other hand, asserts her right as woman and citizen to create her own relation to the nation, to family, and to language against traditions that use gender to mark the limits of the woman's contribution to the nation. Speaking aggressively against cultural and ideological pressures that restrict their public identity, these women claim public voices by appropriating for their own purposes a genre that has long supported traditional forms of male identity. As Sidonie Smith argues, "the mythologies of gender conflate human and male figures of selfhood, aligning male selfhood with culturally valued stories. Autobiography is itself one of the forms of selfhood constituting the idea of man and in turn promoting that idea." The woman who chooses to write autobiography, therefore, "unmasks her transgressive desire for cultural and literary authority" (*Poetics*, 50). If, as Smith suggests, women who write autobiography reveal a desire to transgress cultural norms, they reveal additional transgressive desires when the autobiographies in question challenge the forms of national as well as gender identity. Nonetheless, not every woman's autobiography effectively challenges tradition or leads to new and liberating conceptions of self and nation. Consequently, several of the texts that I discuss are narratives of disappointed desire in which the burden of political and economic realities crush the aspiration for a more equitably imagined national community.

At the same time, we should note that it is not only the female autobiographers who face confining models of selfhood. In this regard, one of the most interesting features of the texts that I read here is their variety. Some of the women's texts demonstrate a clear reluctance to identify with other women, whereas some of the men move toward an identity based in groups rather than on the individual. A similar pattern is evident in the ways that these autobiographers portray national identity. Whereas certain women claim full identity and citizenship, at least one of the men describes the ways that the nation rebuffs his best efforts at identifying himself through it. My point is simply that the nine autobiographies that I discuss do not support broad generalizations in terms of gendered response to the nation or to autobiographical norms of identity. Whatever uniformity there is in these narratives comes from the belief in the ability to reimagine the nation rather than from rigidly gendered responses to it.

Reading the nine autobiographers whom I discuss in terms of the freedom that they claim in order to shape their own relationship to the nation is less an existentialist statement than an interpretation of an autobiographical strategy. Whatever the irrecoverable "reality" of their experiences may have been, the re-presentation of those experiences as autobiographical narratives requires that these writers *stage* themselves and their use of nation. This staging or literary creation of self allows them to assert some degree of autonomy from the nation or, on the other hand, to emphasize the nation's power to mold the individual—all in the process of creating a literary text. It is, in other words, the autobiographer's portrayal of his or her relation to the imagined community that is at question rather than freedom. The simple fact that lived experience, whether it is torture, hunger, or something as mild as a tour of Rome, must be remembered and then expressed in language means that there is nothing but language in autobiography. In this regard, there is no difference between the narratives of Rigoberta Menchú and Richard Rodriguez (two texts that are otherwise fundamentally opposed in their approach to language, to the nation, and in terms of the effect that they seek to produce on the reader and on the world). These two figures stand at opposite ends of the spectrum in terms of style as well as in the safety or danger that they experience in their countries, but the unpolished Spanish of Menchú is no more immediate—that is to say, it grants the reader no greater access to her experience—than does the highly stylized English prose of Rodriguez. Ana María Amar Sánchez has written on this important point, observing that "non-fiction accounts—testimonial narratives—are not simply transcriptions of more or less significant events; on the contrary, they raise a number of theoretical problems due to the peculiar relation that they establish between reality and fiction, the testimonial and its narrative construction. . . . they are not a 'repetition' of reality, but they constitute a new reality governed by its own laws, with which the 'verisimilitude' of other versions is denounced" ("Ficción," 447; my translation). I acknowledge the fact that autobiographical writing is a mediated and fictionalized portrayal of experience—a new reality—rather than the experience itself, but I am not particularly concerned with the much-discussed disappearance of the autobiographical subject. Arguing for that disappearance in what has become the classic statement of poststructuralist criticism on autobiography, Paul de Man asks:

> We assume that life *produces* the autobiography as an act produces its consequences, but can we not suggest, with equal justice, that the autobiographical project may itself produce and determine the life and that whatever the writer *does* is in fact governed by the technical demands of self-portraiture and thus determined, in all its aspects, by the resources of his medium? And since the mimesis here assumed to be operative is one mode of figuration among others, does the referent determine the figure, or is it the other way round: is the illusion of reference not a correlation of the structure of the figure, that is to say no longer clearly and simply a referent at all but something more akin to a fiction which then, however, in its own turn, acquires a degree of referential productivity? ("De-facement," 920–21)

I follow Philippe Lejeune's lead in recognizing the profound shift in our understanding of autobiography that this statement represents, but like Lejeune, I find autobiographers' efforts to communicate experience compelling, even though the "referential productivity" that makes communication happen is a fiction. I cite Lejeune against de Man because the position that Lejeune outlines strikes me as particularly helpful as I frame my reading of autobiographical writing via the nation. Combining awareness of poststructuralist theory with his response to it, Lejeune says:

> It's better to get on with confessions: yes, I have been fooled. I believe that we can promise to tell the truth; I believe in the transparency of language, and in the existence of a complete subject who expresses himself through it . . . I believe that when I say "I," it is I who am speaking: I believe in the Holy Ghost of the first person. And who doesn't believe in it? But it also happens that I believe the contrary, or at least claim to believe it. Whence the fascination that *Roland Barthes par Roland Barthes* . . . has held for me; it . . . proposes a dizzying game of lucidity around all the presuppositions of autobiographical discourse—so dizzying that it ends up giving the reader the illusion that it is not doing what it is nevertheless doing. "In the field of the subject, there is no referent." To a lesser degree, and more candidly, many autobiographers have outlined analogous strategies. We *indeed know* all this; we are not so dumb, but, once this precaution has been taken, we go on as if we did not know it. Telling the truth about the self, constituting the self as complete subject—it is a fantasy. In spite of the fact that autobiography is impossible, this in no way prevents it from existing. (*On Autobiography*, 131–32)

With Lejeune, I believe that despite the slippages, lacunae, and aporias of language, we can communicate the story of the self—fragmented, contingent, and constructed though it may be.

Whatever our critical misgivings regarding the autonomy of the subject or the capacity of language to refer to anything but itself, and in spite of what is ultimately the fantasy of autobiography, writers continue to produce autobiographies to create and express identity and, as in the narratives considered here, to work out what is most often a syncretic relationship between the individual, language, family, class, and the nation. Readers, meanwhile, continue to purchase and read those narratives. Although the profoundly ambiguous nature of autobiography may ultimately leave the reader with nothing but de Man's "illusion of reference," that illusion is nonetheless the central feature of an autobiographical discourse that continues to thrive and mutate. The reader and critic of autobiography can therefore choose between, among others, approaches that emphasize the fictive and self-referential nature of autobiography and reading strategies that concentrate on the autobiographer's attempt to communicate a vision of his or her place in the world. It is, in short, a choice between what Georg Gugelberger calls the "virtual reality games" of deconstructive readings of *testimonio* and readings that recognize the unstable and fictive nature of texts that nonetheless communicate and thus act in the world ("Institutionalization," 10).

G. Thomas Couser's metaphor of the "dot-matrix 'I'" suggests an intriguing combination of these critical stances. According to Couser, "we seem to have entered the age of the dot-matrix 'I': that crucial personal pronoun, once impressed on the page by an integral piece of type, is now merely a particular configuration of the otherwise indistinguishable dots that serve to make up all the other characters. (Indeed, as 'I' write this, 'I' am even less substantial than a constellation of dots mechanically imprinted on a page of paper: 'I' consists of pixels dancing on a video screen. The steadiness of my image is an illusion produced by the speed of the scanning beam)" (*Altered Egos*, 18). Much as de Man claims that we have only the illusion of reference in autobiography, Couser emphasizes the unstable and illusory quality of the autobiographical "I." However, Couser's image cuts both ways. It may well be true that the self is not stable or autonomous, but much as we can read a dot-matrix "I" even though it is composed of dozens of separate and otherwise unrelated dots, even a fragmented self expresses a sense of identity. To paraphrase Lejeune, in spite of the fact that it is impossible to tell the story of the self in the nation, this in no way prevents these nine autobiographies from existing. Similarly, that impossibility in no way prevents us from reading those narratives as attempts to give witness, advance revolution, and create identity.

Realizing that I am not reading reality itself but fictions of memory, language, and sometimes feigned loyalties, I read these autobiographies as efforts to act in the world through the imperfect medium of language. In each case, the nation and the sense of national belonging figure prominently in the autobiographer's sense of self. I use Anderson's "imagined communities" in the chapters that follow as a metaphor for a range of responses to the nation. The autobiographers imagine their communities with such key forces or concepts as the state, ethnicity, gender, class, ideology, migration, and language directing the general outlines that nation takes in each instance.

In chapter 1, I discuss Rigoberta Menchú's *testimonio* in terms of the conflict between her conception of the Quiché Maya nation and the Guatemalan state, emphasizing the resolution of that conflict through an invented tradition—her hybrid ethnic identity. Menchú's presentation of a newly imagined community as if it were a traditional or ancestral society highlights the liberation and instability inherent in Anderson's conception of the nation. If, as Anderson would have it, the image of national communion lives in individual minds, we can expect less communion than subversion when the downtrodden speak against their oppressors.

In chapter 2, I investigate the role of gender in the creation of national identity. My concern here is with the access (or lack of it) that women claim to the nation and with what they portray as their emotional attachment to (or distance from) the nation versus their loyalty to (or hatred for) the state. Through their narratives, Maria Campbell, Carolina Maria de Jesus, and Domitila Barrios de Chungara intervene in the otherwise male nation by imagining their own versions of the national community to claim, with varied success, a space for themselves as women and as citizens.

In chapter 3, I explore the strategic use of myths of national identity to bolster the success of revolutionary movements as presented in the autobiographies of Pierre Vallières and Omar Cabezas. Although nationalism is always an ideological construct, it is consciously ideological for Cabezas and Vallières. These men present their imagined communities with a wink, as it were, manipulating popular cultural images of the nation to conflate the nation and the version of the state that they back as Marxist revolutionaries.

Chapter 4 shifts to a discussion of ethnicity and national belonging in the autobiographies of two children of immigrants: Victor Perera and Maxine Hong Kingston. The questions here center on generational conflicts and on the hard-won version of the imagined community that they produce. Perera's and Kingston's discussions of national belonging or its lack show that when we imagine our community, we necessarily exclude some who are in that community, even as we include others. These autobiographers show that this power to define the nation by excluding is central to the sense of national belonging.

Chapter 5 is dedicated to questions regarding the freedom to choose one's national community. The pressures to conform to tradition and to align oneself with a specific group appear prominently in Richard Rodriguez's *Hunger of Memory*, but in his *Days of Obligation* these questions take on a more directly national focus. I find in Rodriguez's famously contrary positions on ethnicity and language an extreme version of the subjective possibilities inherent in the imagined community. Rodriguez imagines nation in so exclusively individualistic terms as to eliminate the possibility and political relevance of community.

1

Rigoberta Menchú and Survival Culture in Guatemala

The Norwegian Nobel Committee announced on 16 October 1992 that the Nobel Peace Prize would be awarded to Rigoberta Menchú, a Quiché Maya from Guatemala and an advocate for the rights of indigenous peoples. In announcing the prize, the Nobel Committee characterized the new laureate as follows: "Today, Rigoberta Menchú stands out as a vivid symbol of peace and reconciliation across ethnic, cultural and social dividing lines, in her own country, on the American continent and in the world" ("Announcement," 5).

As noted by the Nobel Committee, Menchú's struggle for indigenous rights proceeds through reconciliation of opposing political and cultural forces. While political negotiation constitutes the public portion of this process, an internal—and deeply problematic—reconciliation appears in Menchú's syncretic identity.[1] The chief elements of that combination are the "ladino," or Hispanic, culture of the Guatemalan nation and the Quiché culture of Rigoberta Menchú's people. Several critics of Menchú's 1983 work *Me llamo Rigoberta Menchú y así me nació la conciencia* (*MLRM*), her "as-told-to" autobiography edited by Elizabeth Burgos, which appeared in English in 1984 as *I, Rigoberta Menchú: An Indian Woman in Guatemala*, have commented on the heterogeneous identity and the resulting questions of authenticity produced by the mixture of these elements. Doris Sommer, for example, in her discussion of the discourses and ideologies that Menchú employs, refers to the "multiple unorthodoxies" of the combination ("Rigoberta's Secrets," 46). Other critics, however, are less concerned with these ideological conflicts. Stacey Schlau argues that by refusing to reveal her secrets, Menchú "maintains cultural integrity and distance from the enslaving European culture" ("Rigoberta Menchú," 265), and Pamela Smorkaloff claims that Menchú learns Spanish without suffering alienation from her own culture. "Without losing the ability to think in and as a Quiché, she communicates with the international reading public in Spanish; she learns Spanish as a weapon to defend and preserve her cultural and philosophical Quiché heritage and, by extension, that of all indigenous communities in equal circumstances" ("Crónicas," 113; my translation). Smorkaloff's proposal of Menchú's unity with tradition and culture—not to mention her alleged unity with all indigenous peoples—is highly problematic given the challenge that contact with outside influences presents to traditional ideology. Nonetheless, by defiantly presenting herself as a representative figure, Menchú herself encourages her reader to consider those influences political tools that have been seamlessly absorbed into an enduring Indian identity rather than as evidence of change and difference. I see the rush to insist on authenticity on the part of Menchú as well as many of her readers as much more interesting than the alleged authenticity itself. As I read it, a central concern in *Me llamo Rigoberta Menchú* is the staging of what María Josefina Saldaña Portillo calls the "authentic indigenous other" in relation to both nation and state ("Re-guarding Myself," 90).

The outside influences that Menchú confronts and then absorbs include ideological forces such as language, religion, and political philosophy; she must also face the violence that the Guatemalan *state* uses to enforce its claim to represent a Guatemalan *nation*. In a discussion of the plight of the Mayan peoples of Guatemala, W. George Lovell makes it clear that Rigoberta Menchú and her community do not face the challenge of a violent government alone:

> An estimated one million Indians (one Maya in four) fled or were displaced from their homes between 1981 and 1985 as a result of counterinsurgency tactics. Among those displaced, some sought refuge in the forests and mountains surrounding their gutted communities, where they wandered for months in search of food and shelter. Others drifted to the squatter settlements of Guatemala City, discarding their

native garb and Maya tongue in an effort to "ladinoize" and stay
alive. Still others, pushed beyond the limits of endurance, moved into
the guerrilla fold, took up arms, and are now fighting back. ("Surviving Conquest," 47)

Although the challenge of state violence is not unique to Menchú and her
people, her response through a new imagination of an ancestral national
community represents a distinctly personal contribution. Against the brutality of the Guatemalan state and from a position no longer within tradition and community, Menchú reclaims nation by narrating the invention of a new tradition in the interest of survival.

Benedict Anderson defines the nation as "an imagined political community . . . imagined as both inherently limited and sovereign," explaining his use of "community" when he argues that "regardless of the actual
inequality and exploitation that may prevail in each, the nation is always
conceived as a deep, horizontal comradeship" (*IC*, 6, 7). This comradeship must be imagined, as mentioned, since "the members of even the
smallest nation will never know most of their fellow-members, meet them,
or even hear of them" (6). To support the idea that the sharing of an imagined comradeship forms the nation, Anderson quotes Ernst Renan, who
suggests that the citizens of a nation jointly forget the violence of the past:
"Yet the essence of a nation is that all individuals have many things in
common, and also that they have forgotten many things. . . . every French
citizen has to have forgotten the massacre of Saint Bartholomew, or the
massacre that took place in the Midi in the thirteenth century" ("What
Is a Nation," 11).

While an imagined comradeship and a tacit agreement to forget may
exist elsewhere, Rigoberta Menchú argues that indigenous people cannot
forget the violence that created and still sustains Guatemala. Quite the
contrary; rather than share a forgetting, she and her people insist that
Guatemala remember and acknowledge the brutality that it has perpetrated against her family and her people in the name of the nation. The
simple fact that Menchú and her people occupy the position of the forgotten but always remembering victims rather than that of the forgetting
victors makes dramatically clear the subversive power of a new national
community imagined against the Guatemalan state.

The conflicts between the state and the locally imagined nation that
Menchú narrates demonstrate the weakness in Anderson's theory of the
imagined community that I discuss in my introduction. Anthony Smith
takes issue with Anderson, suggesting that the flaw with this conception

of the nation is that "any self-selecting group, provided its aspirations are spatially limited, can claim to be a nation," and he goes on to list the "common ideas and motifs" of the "ideal type" of the nation ("Problem," 380–81). Menchú's text requires an understanding of nation that modifies both Smith and Anderson. Smith's language suggests a need to regulate nations by carefully limiting the number of peoples honored with the title. Anderson, on the other hand, deals most explicitly with those who forget their own crimes to forge the nation rather than with those whose oppression keeps them out of that nation. Menchú's text requires the reader to adopt a new frame of reference in which the neglected and the oppressed can speak both as a separate nation and against a hegemonic state whose rhetoric would subsume them in a multiethnic and national project.

I should emphasize here the significant but often overlooked difference between the nation and the state. The nation is, in Xavier Arbós's terms, "a human group, whose members consider themselves as a nation because of some distinctive cultural features" ("Nation-State," 61–62). "Nation" is a culturally descriptive term; it refers to a sense of distinctness held by members of a group whose sense of cohesion is linked to either possession of or claims to a geographical area. The state, on the other hand, is a political entity that regulates the affairs of the people or peoples, nation or nations, within its borders. Nationalist struggles are frequently rooted in the fact that in only a few cases are nation and the state used to describe the same piece of ground, and in the subsequent desire of various ethnic and cultural groups for correspondence between nation and state. William Lawton notes: "The ideal conception of the nation-state is a political unit whose boundaries are coterminous with those of an ethnic group; the theory of and desire for such a political unit is the essence of modern ethnic nationalism" ("Crisis," 134).

Me llamo Rigoberta Menchú details the abuses that have followed the establishment of a state that is anything but coterminous with nation. A major emphasis of Menchú's text is her critique of the idea that living within a border justifies the assumption of community or shared nationality. By explaining the systematic marginalization of unassimilated indigenous peoples, and by narrating the violence through which they are excluded from the political processes of the state, Rigoberta Menchú demonstrates the fundamental illegitimacy of Guatemala as a political body. Diane Nelson comments on the crisis of the nation-state in Guatemala with specific reference to Menchú:

Rigoberta Menchú's Nobel Peace Prize and the resistance to the
Columbus Quincentenary have forced the country's internal ethnic
differences (some 60% of Guatemala's population is indigenous,
divided into over 20 ethno-linguistic groups) into the public consciousness, foregrounding what is seen as a failure of nation. In much
of the discussion, this lack of a seamless national identity suited for
participation in the "modern" inter-national world is blamed on the
survival of pre-modern, locally-based ethnic identity onto a seemingly
autonomous Mayan population. ("Gendering," 4)

Much of Menchú's narrative is indeed focused on divisions between the
ladino and indigenous populations and on the brutality suffered by the
many Guatemalan Maya peoples. However, her critique of Guatemala reveals much more than the expected crimes of an oppressive state. Despite
the insistence that she belongs to an ancient and traditional culture or a
separate nation, close reading reveals that Quiché culture as presented in
Me llamo Rigoberta Menchú is a recent creation, an imagined community
formed in the interest of surviving governmental assault.

The military and ideological aspects of state violence against that
community are made abundantly clear throughout the narrative. For example, the thrust of the following passage is that the opposition between
indigenous and ladino Guatemala represents more than a response by
the Indians to Hispanic culture. Menchú contends that this opposition
excludes the Indian from the political and social life of the Guatemalan
state and therefore from the nation that the state claims to represent.
"But we realized that in Guatemala there is something greater and something smaller, and that's what we are. That the ladinos behave like a su-
perior race. There was a time in which they say that the ladinos doubted
that we were even people. That we were some kind of animal. I was able
to settle all this in my mind. That was how it was when I gave myself
to the struggle and said to myself that we had to overthrow the enemy"
(*MLRM*, 149).

Commenting on this use of native peoples to define the nonnative nation, Nelson notes that "there is a *need* for difference which extends from
national subjects' demands for a self-consolidating other to the history
of Guatemala's economic development which has depended on the super-
exploitation of the indigenous 'other'" ("Gendering," 4).

That this ideological move to classify the Indian as the "other" of Hispanic Guatemala goes hand in hand with the definition of the Indian as a
noncitizen becomes unmistakably clear in the most graphically violent sec-

tion of the narrative. In these pages soldiers of the Guatemalan army compel the residents of several villages to view the tortured bodies of captured Indians, among whom is the brother of Rigoberta Menchú, Petrocinio. Introducing the grim spectacle, Menchú observes: "It's that the government gave us, to my family, an image as if we were monsters, *as if we were foreigners.* But my father was Quiché, he wasn't Cuban" (MLRM, 198; emphasis added). Since the point of the soldiers' questions is national allegiance, it is enormously significant that Menchú identifies her father as Quiché, loyal to the Quiché people, rather than as *guatemalteco*, loyal to Guatemala. If it was not evident before, it must be now that Menchú and her people do not consider themselves part of the Guatemalan nation and, consequently, do not recognize the authority of the Guatemalan state. The government realizes this but reinforces the separation with its response. As the military official in charge of the operation displays the gruesomely abused bodies—"we saw the monstrous and unrecognizable faces" (202)—we see just what kind of "horizontal comradeship" there is between the government and the indigenous peoples of Guatemala. "That's what you get for being communists! [¡Eso es por ser comunistas!] For being Cubans, for being subversives!" (202).

> It was impossible to think straight, to actually see that happening.
> You had to think that they were human beings and what pain those
> bodies would have felt to reach the point of being unrecognizable. . . .
> During the speech the captain kept saying that our government was
> democratic and that it gave us everything. What more did we want?
> That the subversives brought in foreign ideas, strange ideas that led
> us to torture and he pointed to the bodies of the men. And that if we
> took orders from foreigners we would die just as they were going to.
> (204)

After the victims, still only half-dead, are doused with gasoline and set on fire, the soldiers drive off, shouting their final insult: "Long live the fatherland! Long live Guatemala! Long live our president! Long live the army!" (205). The point of the public executions could not be more starkly obvious: the Guatemalan nation lives by violently excluding and repressing the indigenous population.

In his study of contemporary Guatemalan history, *Unfinished Conquest: The Guatemalan Tragedy*, Victor Perera (whose autobiography I discuss in chapter 4) does not directly refute Menchú's testimony, but he does provide evidence that contradicts some of the details of this episode. Referring to accounts of the massacre that differ in some aspects from

Menchú's, Perera concludes: "Although these discrepancies are not read-ily accounted for, Rigoberta Menchú's testimony is entirely consistent with other eyewitness accounts of torture, burnings, and mass executions that I have gathered myself" (*Unfinished Conquest*, 106). The possibility that Menchú may not have witnessed this or other events or that she may have blurred details is troubling, as evident in Perera's haste to reconcile the dis-crepancies. However, while our ability to verify the "facts" of an autobi-ography may have a great deal to do with its value as history, that ability has little connection to its value as a subjective portrayal of collective ex-perience. The description of the murder of her brother may be a compi-lation of similar outrages given expression as a representative case. For my purposes, the historicity of the event is less important than the use to which Menchú puts it.

Although specific details may invite controversy, the fact of the mur-derous brutality suffered by the indigenous majority of Guatemala is be-yond dispute. Given that savagery, the decision to suspend identification with ancestral culture becomes the only way to save lives. Nonetheless, the choice to submit culture to the demands of survival is neither auto-matic nor easy. It is a difficult decision that would have been impossible without the ability to replace tradition by imagining a new community and identity. The creation of this new sense of self as part of a tradition fashioned in the interest of survival frees Menchú from the no-win choice between inaction and certain destruction or action and the hope of im-provement at the price of a loss of cultural identification. Had she and her people been unable to imagine a new group identity, they would have necessarily already lost the battle since culture, Quiché culture in partic-ular, exists in constant flux. As Lovell observes, since a return to a pre-Columbian life was impossible after the conquest, Mayan society became "a creative blend of elements of Hispanic culture the Maya had absorbed, mixed with elements of pre-Columbian culture they had defended and up-held" ("Surviving Conquest," 32). As her ancestors have done since the arrival of the Spaniards, Rigoberta Menchú presents an innovative and hybrid community as if it were traditional by bridging the demands of sur-vival and the desire for cultural continuity. It is not the return to tradi-tion that counts but the rhetoric surrounding and giving meaning to that strategy. As Neil ten Kortenaar has said of the politics of culture and au-thenticity, "one may not be able to return to the world of one's ancestors, but one can claim to be doing so, with political effect. Tradition has an ontological existence, not in the past but in the present, where it affects people's self-images and their behavior" ("Beyond Authenticity," 40). Neither Menchú nor anyone else can return to the past. She and her people can, however, claim to return to the traditions and practices of the past and thus shield themselves against a modern world that seeks to devour them. The resulting "authentic" indigenous identity is less a sign of connection with the past than an innovative manipulation of the past for purposes solidly grounded in the political demands of the present. Saldaña Portillo observes, "if Menchú does not frame the spectacle of her own [political] transformation, she does, on the other hand, frame the spectacle of her Quiché culture as 'authentic.' This 'spectacle' then forms the basis for political struggle" ("Re-guarding Myself," 94).

Not even the spectacle of authentic culture, however, is stable since Menchú presents herself as both a cultural innovator and a defender of tradition. With her decision that innovation provides her only hope for survival comes a growing lack of confidence in Quiché culture that reinforces her decision to adopt elements of foreign cultures. This erosion of cultural ground and confidence has two important components: the accumulation of alien values violates repeated warnings found in "traditional" culture against mixing with the ladinos—itself an unrecognized innovation; and, in order to accommodate new ideologies and to ease the internal conflict provoked by the transgression of cultural norms, Menchú suspends belief in the practices and beliefs that characterize that traditional culture. Once this suspension has been accomplished, values become fluid. Menchú defends not a culture, nor a way of life, nor a political program— she defends life and human rights. Contrary to readings that find in *Me llamo Rigoberta Menchú* a revolutionary practice that preserves traditional culture, I find in these mixed cultures evidence of eroded confidence in traditional cultural values and, paradoxically, the creation of an "invented tradition." Eric Hobsbawm explains that invented traditions are "responses to novel situations which take the form of reference to old situations" ("Inventing Traditions," 2), a pattern that Menchú follows closely as she creates a new authentic past from which she can draw validation and to which she can claim loyalty.

The creation of an invented tradition from foreign practices and ideologies becomes necessary when governmental aggression threatens cultural and physical existence. In order to survive this onslaught, Rigoberta Menchú pulls into her cultural arsenal anything that preserves life. This flexible strategy contrasts sharply with the rigid ideological training that she details in the early chapters of *Me llamo Rigoberta Menchú*. I use the term "ideological" to emphasize that, whatever their motives, the elders of the community enforce and seek to perpetuate an interpretation of the world and of proper action in it. In this instance, ideology resembles the second and third of Terry Eagleton's six definitions of the term in his *Ideology: An Introduction*. Eagleton states that ideology "turns on ideas and beliefs (whether true or false) which symbolize the conditions and life-experiences of a specific, socially significant group or class" and, later, that it concerns "the *promotion* and *legitimation* of the interests of such social groups in the face of opposing interests" (*Ideology*, 29). These aspects of ideology are present in *Me llamo Rigoberta Menchú* in, among other places, a kind of christening ritual during which the infant receives the following charge: "After this he will multiply our race, that child will replace all those who have died. That is when the child accepts the responsibility. And that is when he is told that he has to live as his ancestors lived" (*MLRM*, 34). The fear of outside influences entering the community matches the fear of departing from the community expressed in the prohibition against exceeding established boundaries. These fears prompt Menchú's father, Vicente Menchú, to counsel her against attending Spanish-speaking schools. "He always said, 'Unfortunately, if I put you in school, they are going to make you forget your class origins, they are going to make you into a ladino, and I don't want that for you and that's why I don't send you'" (216).

Menchú's need to position herself as at once within and without her community, as at once traditional and highly innovative, as Kristeva's woman at the crossing of boundaries, highlights the unstable nature of her narrative. As I read them, the conflicts and contradictions of the text are as much a part of the message as they are part of the medium through which the message is expressed. Unless we are to practice a criticism preoccupied with the impossibility of communicating realities through language, we must attend to the grim facts that appear throughout *Me llamo Rigoberta Menchú*. Nonetheless, such attention need not imply turning a blind eye to ideological difficulties. This narrative is produced by a woman with as many fears, insecurities, biases, and unspoken motivations as strengths. This is also a woman who speaks for a group from which she has become quite different. The differences between the representative and the represented are certainly as much a part of the text as the scenes of abuse, and they strike me as ultimately more painful since they represent the times Menchú feels compelled to loosen cultural ties in the interest of survival. R. Todd Wise speaks of our moral, political, and intellectual reactions to these scenes and to the entire narrative when he reminds us that "the postmodern reader must not only acknowledge signs and codes but experience the clenched fist, the tight neck, and the sick feeling in the stomach when faced with the suffering other" ("Native American," 117). The combination—clenched fists *and* acknowledgment of signs and codes—means that we cannot content ourselves with an insistence that *testimonio* presents the "real" and the "historical." Since the effort to construct that reality and that history is a central issue in *Me llamo Rigoberta Menchú*, tight necks and clenched fists must not preclude careful attention to the political interests and ideological contests at play in the creation of a people's history through an individual's life story.

As Menchú creates that history, one of her aims is to connect contemporary practices and beliefs with ancestral traditions. In one instance of this effort, she gives concrete expression to the ideological imperatives of purity and separation by contrasting the bread of the *conquistadores* with the tortillas of the ancient and contemporary Maya. The Quiché reject the bread of Hispanic culture because it is a mixture, but accept the tortilla because it is made of corn alone. The images of compound bread and pure tortillas lead directly to a denunciation of racial mixing. "Later, the bread, they say, the bread has great significance for the Indian. The fact that bread is mixed with egg, flour with egg. Before, our ancestors grew wheat. The Spaniards came and mixed egg with it. Now it is all mixed up, it is no longer what our ancestors had. This is food of the whites and the whites are just like bread, because they are mixed up too. The blood of our greatest grandparents was joined with the blood of the whites. They are mixed, just like their food" (*MLRM*, 97). That Quiché culture should reject the racial mixture that was forced on it should surprise no one. It is surprising, however, that condemnations of cultural and racial blending should accumulate even as Menchú narrates profound change and innovation. The tension between these conflicting directions produces serious anxiety in Menchú. Concerning the conflict between Menchú's survival strategies and the ideological directive to avoid mixture, Doris Sommer observes that Menchú "must engage in political activity outside the community and its codes and so bear a burden of inevitable contradiction, nostalgia, and hints of guilt" ("Not Just Personal," 127). The very choices that give her a public voice make Menchú different from those for whom she wants to speak, and her feelings of guilt over that difference become apparent as she moves from the condemnation of bread and racial mixture to a criticism of those that transgress cultural norms.

This criticism focuses on the transformation that exposure to other cultures brings to the individual. The transformation metaphorically parallels the journey from the highlands to the coastal plantations that Rigoberta Menchú and thousands like her are forced to make. As Menchú and

her family move from an environment that is initially one of relative stability—albeit one of poverty—to one of filth and degradation, they move
from their homelands to Guatemala. In other words, the journey moves
the Indian from a region in which a kind of ancestral culture can be prac-
ticed to an area in which the violence and power of ladino Guatemala are
all too depressingly present; in spatial terms, it is a descent from the
Quiché nation into the Guatemalan state. As evidence of the debasing
transformation that follows this descent, Menchú offers the example of
the *indígenas ladinizados* who work for the landowners and in the process
become like them. "When we say 'ladinoized' it means that person now
has the attitude of the ladino, and of the bad ladino because we later realized that not all the ladinos are bad. A bad ladino who knows how to
talk and how to rip people off. In other words, he's just like a mini-
landowner" (*MLRM*, 46).

Much as she condemns those who work as foremen for the landown-
ing ladinos, Menchú criticizes women that prostitute themselves as much
for cultural mixing as for their sexual promiscuity. She says, "that's when
prostitutes start to appear because among the Indians we don't have prostitution in our culture, in our customs that we still preserve" (*MLRM*, 58).
The promiscuity that most disturbs Rigoberta Menchú is the willingness
of Quiché men and women to surrender traditional norms for the promise of relative wealth and acceptance in Hispanic culture. If cultural values become fluid for Menchú, this does not imply that "anything goes."
Those who abandon community for selfish reasons degrade themselves
and their people; those who loosen ties to the past in the interest of survival create tradition.

Menchú locates the source of prostitution and homosexuality in the
same contaminating source—Hispanic society. In the case of homosexuals, however, she offers a curiously ambivalent analysis. After presenting
the problem of homosexuals in the community, she argues that these men
are not rejected by her people as they would be among ladinos. Nonetheless, she undercuts this softening of her criticism by identifying homosexuality as a social ill that comes from contact with external culture. "We
don't distinguish between a man who is homosexual and a man who isn't
homosexual because that is something that happens when one goes down
to other places" (*MLRM*, 86). Menchú suggests that in the context of
Quiché cultural values, the distinction cannot be made between homosexuals and heterosexuals because homosexual men must have been lost
to ladino culture in the first place. This position is only confused by the
further claim that Quiché culture considers homosexuality simply another

part of nature. "The good thing with us is that we consider everything to be part of nature. So, for example, a baby animal that didn't come out right, that's part of nature just like a harvest that didn't yield much; we say that you shouldn't hope for more than you can get. It's something that comes with the ladino. A phenomenon that comes with foreign things" (86). Although there may be some sense in which comparison to birth defects and crop failures expresses acceptance of homosexuality, it is difficult to see how this might work.

It seems more likely that Menchú has inadvertently provided an illustration of the tensions and conflicts in her thinking. Through her contact with Western culture, she has learned to accept homosexuality. Later, as she describes Quiché attitudes to Elizabeth Burgos, the ethnographer who records and edits the narrative, Menchú attempts to combine Western and traditional beliefs with the jarring comparison of homosexuals to phenomena like birth defects. Although she does not identify it as such, this mixed thinking seems to illustrate the separation from her origins that develops throughout the text. We see the effects of that separation again in what Menchú portrays as her inability to correctly perceive the political dangers and options of her community. "In shame I expressed my doubts because many others of my community understood better than I did because their minds were very healthy because they had never left the community. We've all gone down to the plantations but they've never had such a distraction as I have. The fact that I have driven around the capital in a bus, for example, that's a little change that an Indian suffers internally. So, my little brothers, my brothers, understood better than I did" (*MLRM*, 147). The presumed response of the ancestors to modern changes makes it clear that the "little change" is anything but a small matter; Menchú supposes that her "ancestors must be shocked to see all these modern things" (29). Given that she acknowledges distance from the culture that she claims to represent, and given that she recognizes in herself a "woman viewed with suspicion by the community" (86), Menchú's decision to loosen cultural ties clearly inspires feelings of guilt and unease.

Four passages locate her decision to depart from tradition in the context of collective decisions. Menchú does not identify the speaker in any of the passages, attributing the responsibility for the conclusions to the community. "*Dejemos las costumbres*," the first passage begins. "Let's leave our customs, our ceremonies, and let's plan for our security first; then everything that we want to do will come later. . . . Now comrades, nobody will discover the secret of our community" (*MLRM*, 151), the decision being to temporarily abandon some cultural practices in order to preserve the secrets of the community. The second passage continues this plan, informing the reader that at one point Menchú's community broke with "many cultural patterns . . . taking into account that it was a way to save ourselves" (154). The third passage also emphasizes the preservation of life, but in this case cultural secrets shift abruptly from primary to secondary importance. "So, we saw the great need to put that [plan] into action because life was the most important thing, even if they were to discover many of our Indian secrets" (170). Similarly, according to the fourth passage, it is more important to keep the members of the community alive than to defend secrets. "That is why when it is a matter of defending our lives, we are willing to defend them even if we have to reveal our secrets" (196). This statement suggests that culture has no special claim to truth. Rather than think of culture in transcendental terms, Rigoberta Menchú views the practices, beliefs, and traditions of her people as responses to the world that are valuable inasmuch as they increase security. When they do not increase security or preserve life, they must be abandoned.

Doris Sommer comments on the constructed nature and vulnerability of Quiché culture, noting that the community leaders "recognize that Indian identity is a fragile cultural-linguistic construction, not an indelibly 'racial' given" ("Rigoberta's Secrets," 35). Sommer rightly attributes an awareness of the fragility of cultural identity to Menchú and her people, but if the community leaders who warn against violating traditional norms recognize that identity is not a matter of blood, they nonetheless insist that there is a proper way to be, even if that "way" is less than biological. The repeated warnings against learning Spanish and mingling with Hispanic Guatemalans, for example, remind us that if identity can be constructed, it can also be changed. A changed identity, in the language of these community elders, is a lost identity. Perhaps influenced as much by the anxieties of her elders regarding the dangerous consequences of cultural mixing as by contact with external ideology, Rigoberta Menchú accepts the conventional nature of cultural values and portrays them, both Quiché and ladino, as relative, contingent truths rather than universal constants. When used in her discussions of culture and tradition, phrases such as *según nuestra cultura* [according to our culture], *es por pura costumbre* [it's just a custom], *para nosotros* [for us], *es más que todo una costumbre* [more than anything, it's just a custom], *como lo decimos nosotros* [as we say], and others like them demonstrate Menchú's understanding of culture as one among many possible interpretations of and responses to life rather than as an inviolable code. This consciousness of the limits of cultural truth eases the concern over violating traditional norms and prepares the way for further modifications. To suggest that Rigoberta Menchú learns to see her people in a broader context is not, however, to suggest that Menchú speaks of her culture objectively after separating herself completely from it. Menchú, like all human beings, is a product of her cultural background and as such cannot simply remove herself from it, but through exposure to other ways of living she gains an appreciation for the fact that there are many ways to understand and to respond to the world.

Since she does not accept cultural values as stable or fixed, Menchú can interpret and use them pragmatically. Those practices and beliefs that work, that defend and preserve life, are maintained. Those that do not serve this most basic purpose are set aside. "We know how to choose the things that really work for our people and those are the things that we put into practice. And that is what has made it possible that we Indians are alive today, because if we didn't, we wouldn't be here" (*MLRM*, 196). With values and practices that work, as with those that do not, a conscious recognition of contingency allows external values that promote the goal of sustaining life to be absorbed as equal to practices and strategies from within Quiché culture. Despite Menchú's anxiety over her departures from ancestral ways, she repeatedly describes how her entire community has made significant adoptions of foreign thinking. At one point, she cites her father's explicit direction to concern herself less with the preservation of culture than with the preservation of life. "My father said very clearly: We don't want any more dead people, we don't want any more martyrs, because there are too many martyrs in our lands, there are too many in our fields that have been killed. So, what we need to do is protect our lives as much as we can and keep up the struggle" (209). Given this guidance, Menchú finally concludes that life must be the central cultural value.

These departures from traditional cultural values are not carried out by Menchú alone, as evident in the extensive mixing of indigenous and Hispanic religion. Catholicism and traditional beliefs mix to such an extent, and have mixed for so long, that it is impossible to separate one from the other in *Me llamo Rigoberta Menchú*. Of the many passages that present the mixture of Catholicism and indigenous religion, the most interesting is the following: "That's how we accommodated it, accepting all that is the Catholic religion and the duty of a Christian *as our culture*. It's not the only stable form to express ourselves but it is a way to continue expressing ourselves and not abandon our way of expressing the beliefs of our ancestors" (*MLRM*, 107; emphasis added). Indigenous culture and European religion blend completely. Menchú even incorporates the Latin liturgy, an apparently easy target for criticism, into Quiché culture. "I remember that at first the prayers weren't even in Spanish. They were in Latin or something like that. So, we feel it but we don't understand what it means. . . . It means a lot to us but we don't understand it" (107). Despite the barriers of language, Menchú makes no distinction between herself, her culture, and her Catholicism. She works for the survival of her people "as a woman, as a Christian, as an Indian" (194), with little apparent concern for the "purity" of any of the three identifying points. Gender, religion, and culture mix to produce a revolutionary Christian whose orthodoxy narrows to a single issue: "The task before revolutionary Christians is more than anything the condemnation, the denunciation of the injustices that are committed against the people" (269).

For Menchú, Christianity is a moral and political force, the natural ally of indigenous peoples in their fight for survival. Since a particular political situation gives rise to this understanding of Christianity and the Bible, those who view Menchú's situation from the outside cannot be expected to understand scripture as do the Quiché. "As I was saying," Menchú comments, "for us the Bible is an important weapon that has taught us how to proceed. And, perhaps, for all those who call themselves Christians, but those who are only Christians in theory don't understand why we give it this meaning precisely because they haven't lived our reality" (159). However, since some priests have learned to see the world as do the dispossessed, she challenges all to find in the Bible the essence of Christianity—the liberation of the oppressed. "We do that precisely because we feel that we are Christians and the duty of a Christian is to find ways to bring about the kingdom of God on the earth with our brothers. The kingdom will exist only when we all have enough to eat. When our children, our brothers, our fathers don't have to die of hunger and malnutrition. That would truly be glorious, a real kingdom for us, because we've never had that. That is very different from what a priest thinks" (15–60).

Near the end of *Me llamo Rigoberta Menchú*, Menchú repeats the contrast between apparent and essential Christianity: "I am a catechist with her feet on the ground and not a catechist who thinks that the kingdom of God is only something for after we die" (*MLRM*, 269). This reading of the Bible as a directive for the establishment of equality through subversion and rebellion lends a potent ambiguity to the idea that her assignment is to organize groups and to share with them "the light of the gospel" (272). We see that Rigoberta Menchú's reading of Christian texts is, like her use of indigenous culture, one of many tools in her syncretic strategy. Much as she suspends belief in traditional culture to allow herself to mingle foreign elements with it, so her use of Christianity is provisional in that she remains open to additional sources of support for her struggle. Similarly, political ideologies require modification and completion. "The world I live in is so evil, so bloody, that from one moment to the next I could be killed. That's why the only alternative I have is the struggle, justified violence, just like I've learned in the Bible. I tried to make a Marxist comrade understand that because she couldn't see how I could support revolution as a Christian. I told her that not all the truth is in the Bible, but that not all the truth was in Marxism either" (271). Among other sources, Rigoberta Menchú turns to Christianity, Marxism, indigenous culture, and the Spanish language for support in her struggle for survival and as elements of an evolving syncretic identity. Speaking of her training in Spanish, Menchú indicates her continuing openness to new and foreign experiences. She says in a 1992 interview: "Spanish has given me the opportunity to know something about the lives and struggles of other peoples, from South Africa to the Amazon. . . . I wish I could speak more languages" ("Quincentenary," 100). The incompleteness of Christianity, Marxism, and Spanish precludes the identification of any of them as the source of ultimate truth, but they are all valuable in that they provide, as she says of Catholicism, "otro canal para expresarse" [another means of expression] (*MLRM*, 29).

Menchú tells her reader that she was instructed to seek out new forms of resistance; nonetheless, a strong sense of guilt accompanies the accumulation of foreign material. As we have seen, part of her response to that guilt becomes apparent in the suspension of confidence in traditional culture. Since she sees cultural values as relative rather than absolute truths, Menchú can use or discard them according to the needs and goals of a given situation. This strategy, although persistent, is not the only response to alienation. Menchú argues that her community retains its traditional and isolated identity in order to authenticate her own indigenous roots, but she needs to demonstrate that others also violate traditional norms. Menchú must create a narrative space for herself as the spokesperson of a united and traditional people even though neither she nor her people are "traditional" if we insist that the term means connection to an unbroken and unchanging past. Her history, like any other, is necessarily a personal and subjective construct that tells us as much about her individual interests and motivations as it does about collective pain.

The adoption of Catholicism provides the most visible instance of the group's deviation from tradition, but the early life of Menchú's father is also an important and forceful departure. In a passage that was ignored in the critical discussion of *Me llamo Rigoberta Menchú* until very recently, we discover that Vicente Menchú, the father of Rigoberta, was given to a white family as a child since there was not enough food to feed him. "He lived with people . . . like . . . white, white people" (*MLRM*, 23). We learn later that Vicente was enrolled in the army. "And so my father went into the military. That is where he learned a lot of bad things and where he also learned to be a complete man because he says that when he got into the service they treated him like any old object and that they trained him with their fists, the main thing that he learned was that military training" (24). Only after the years spent with a white family, only after time spent in the army, only after extended contact with ladino culture, does Vicente establish the village. "That's how they went to the mountains. There was no village. No one was there. They went to found a village in that place" (24–25). Even if the only effect of Vicente Menchú's exposure to Hispanic culture were hatred, it would still be the case that the origins of this community lie in cultural mixture rather than in cultural purity. John Beverley says of this new village:

> Nothing more "post-modern," nothing more traversed by the economic and cultural forces of transnational capitalism . . . than the social, economic, and cultural contingencies Menchú and her family live and die in. Even the communal mountain *aldea*, or village, that the text evokes so compellingly, with its collective rituals and economic life that makes it seem like an ancient Mayan Gemeinschaft that has survived five hundred years of conquest more or less intact, turns out on closer inspection to be a recent settlement. ("Real Thing," 277)

The origins of this little village provide a solution to Menchú's problematic claim to representative status. Most critics of *Me llamo Rigoberta Menchú* have read this claim positively, seeing it in terms of an activist's desire to mobilize a people. However, when Menchú says, "my personal situation encompasses the entire reality of a people" (*MLRM*, 21), we might well consider that Rigoberta Menchú performs individually what the group performs collectively: the conscious departure from tradition in the interest of survival. Her father is sent away, physically expelled from the family to prevent his starvation. Likewise, the community transforms itself, invents a new traditional past to survive. Menchú changes herself in turn by accumulating foreign values and by rearranging traditional values to preserve life and to give voice to the struggle of her people.

Furthermore, as Santiago Colás has argued, it is Menchú's ambiguous position as simultaneous insider and outsider that makes her representative status possible. "The resistance value of the testimonio as cultural practice and artifact, far from resting on either the absolute identity between a people, their representative, the interlocutor, and the foreign symphathizer, seems rather to derive from the tension generated by the disjuncture between these different subjects. It is not the testimonio's uncontaminated positing of some pure, truthful, native history that makes it so powerful, but rather its subversion of such a project" ("What's Wrong," 170). Colás contends that the *testimonialista*, "while undoubtedly inside the community (whatever that might mean since the community is constituted only in the process of that agent's narration), has as the conditions of possibility of his or her speech in the *testimonio* his or her simultaneous exteriority to that community. In short, this agent is not identical to the other members of that community, precisely because he or she has chosen to speak" (165–66). The tension between the representative and the represented that Colás describes is explicit in Menchú's case, and the effects of that tension appear repeatedly in the narrative. Even if such a tension is necessary for representation to occur, it is important to see that the need to emphasize authenticity and compliance with tradition exaggerates this tension dramatically. Had she narrated her story in terms emphasizing the creation of a new culture rather than insisting on the preservation of an ancient culture, there would be less conflict between tradition and innovation, but the simple fact of physical separation through exile (*Me llamo Rigoberta Menchú* was narrated in Paris) would still complicate the representative's relationship to the represented.

Whatever the narrative, political, or cultural benefits of such difference, separation is painful for Menchú. Exposure to other cultures violates admonitions against cultural hybridity, and identity becomes highly problematic since the instructions not to mix cultures and Menchú's commitment to follow those directions appear side by side with evidence of mixing. The Nobel Peace Prize embodies the transformations and the contradictions inherent in this process. Radical changes were necessary before she could gain the visibility required to be considered for such an honor. However, those changes create even more visibility and consequently heightened effectiveness in the effort to defend the indigenous peoples of Guatemala. The prize, in other words, becomes another weapon in the struggle for cultural preservation even as it indicates departure from tradition.

The struggle against Guatemala to which Menchú has given herself is a battle for survival. Confronted on one hand with physical destruction and on the other with cultural annihilation, Rigoberta Menchú and her people have bravely and creatively sought to resist power through the defense of traditional culture and through the selective incorporation of foreign ideologies. In choosing to assimilate external material, Menchú is not alone. Though there are serious difficulties in extrapolating from the lives it narrates to lives and situations across Guatemala, *Me llamo Rigoberta Menchú* provides insight into the grim realities of that nation. The conflict that she narrates between official and popular conceptions of the nation, moreover, prefigures similar contests discussed in later chapters.

2

State, National, and Gender Identity: Maria Campbell, Carolina Maria de Jesus, and Domitila Barrios de Chungara

Rigoberta Menchú's description of the violence perpetrated against her people by the Guatemalan government goes beyond that basic conflict to narrate tensions between the persecuted group and an individual member of that group. This strain complicates the effort to maintain a tradition by exposing the invented and strategic quality of that tradition. The conflict between a portrayal of culture as a set of values subject to criticism and, on the other hand, as a fixed set of rituals and beliefs that have survived centuries of violent opposition and that continue to define the Quiché Maya reveals what culture is and what culture does in *Me llamo Rigoberta Menchú*.

Although culture, either as an ancestral legacy or as an invented tradition, plays a lesser role in the narratives considered in this chapter, a similar tension between the individual and the group controls the sense of self that emerges in the autobiographies of Maria Campbell, Carolina Maria de Jesus, and Domitila Barrios de Chungara. Whether resisting pressure to identify oneself ethnically, lamenting the social inequity produced by a lack of patriotism, or strategically emphasizing class unity to advance a political program, all three women portray themselves vis-à-vis nations and national governments that abuse, neglect, or oppose them as members of the underclass. Excluded, starved, or tortured, these women respond by either rejecting the nation or by calling for a reorganization of the state.

With these three narratives it becomes clear that Santiago Colás's comment on *Me llamo Rigoberta Menchú* applies broadly to testimonial discourse. "The testimonio is more a cause," Colás says, "than an effect, of group identity" ("What's Wrong," 164). Following Colás, we can say that *testimonio* works as the cause of group identity on at least two levels. First, the *testimonio* can lead to a sense of group identity or unity in readers within the national situation described as well as in readers who live far from that situation both geographically and politically. Secondly, these texts might be seen as the cause of group identity if we consider the group-based sense of self as a literary trope. In this case, the *testimonialista* emphasizes group identity as much to fulfill the expectations of readers of the genre as to express a social truth. Alone among these three women, Chungara can portray a plural subject that grows out of an actual political organization. It is that link to a concrete rather than merely desired unity that gives her the confidence to imagine her national community in broadly inclusive and ambitiously egalitarian terms.

My selection of three autobiographical narratives that emphasize exclusion, hunger, and violence highlights the similarities in the material and political conditions that the texts depict. Given the importance of such conditions in these narratives, poverty and oppression must be considered in any discussion of them. However, since these accounts are life stories that portray the formation of individual identity through specific social circumstances, for my purposes the individual responses to conditions are more important than the conditions themselves. My emphasis on the varied responses to similar conditions makes this reading different in purpose from studies such as Lisa Davis's "An Invitation to Understanding among Poor Women of the Americas." Whereas that essay concludes that "there is a unity of vision and experience in the lives of poor women of color across geographic boundaries" (237), I acknowledge similar conditions and then move to an investigation of the ways in which the peculiarities of response shape identity in these autobiographies.

For the purposes of this chapter, it is the degree to which the women associate themselves with or disassociate themselves from their most proximate groups that most powerfully shapes personal and national identity.

There is neither a right nor a wrong way of identifying oneself relative to a group, but traditions, ideals, and political goals lead—or compel—the individual to adopt preestablished forms of identity in relation to family, class, or nation. Because the response to conditions rather than a pre-existing essence creates identity for both individuals and nations, we do well to heed Fredric Jameson's warning against readings of group identity that are not "historicized." "Appeals to collective identity need to be evaluated from a historical perspective," Jameson says, "rather than from the standpoint of some dogmatic and placeless 'ideological analysis.' When a third-world writer invokes this (to us) ideological value, we need to examine the concrete historical situation closely in order to determine the political consequences of the strategic use of this concept" ("Third-World Literature," 78).

Maria Lugones's concepts of "thickness" and "transparency" provide a helpful scheme for describing the ways Campbell, de Jesus, and Chungara portray the strategic relationship between the individual and the group. Lugones describes that correspondence or conflict by saying, "thickness and transparency are group relative. Individuals are transparent with respect to their group if they perceive their needs, interests, ways, as those of the group and if this perception becomes dominant or hegemonical in the group. Individuals are thick if they are aware of their otherness in the group, of their needs, interests, ways, being relegated to the margins in the politics of intragroup contestation. So, as transparent, one becomes unaware of one's own difference from other members of the group" ("Purity," 474).

Importantly, Lugones does not suggest that group and individual identity predate encounters with groups or that group identity is somehow more natural than individual identity. In the descriptive scheme proposed by Lugones, Campbell best exemplifies thickness, given that *Halfbreed* narrates her reluctance to view her needs and interests in terms of those of larger groups such as women, the Métis, or Canada. De Jesus also feels thick relative to her local group, the *favelados*, but regardless of her sense that she differs significantly from her neighbors in the shantytown, she identifies herself specifically and proudly as a Brazilian—as transparent in national terms. Chungara, the most politically active of the three women, portrays herself as transparent relative to the mining families of her community, Siglo XX, to the women of Bolivia, and to Bolivia as a nation.

The serious problems that these women confront highlight the restraint and subjugation in the nation-woman relationship. As Deniz Kandiyoti notes, national ideologies frequently identify women as "privileged bearers of corporate identities and boundary markers" unable to function as "full fledged citizens of modern nation states" ("Identity and Discontents," 441). Julia Kristeva, however, speaks positively of the possibilities inherent in the place women hold in the nation:

> women today are called upon to share in the creation of new social groupings where, by *choice* rather than on account of *origin*, through lucidity rather than fate, we shall try to assure our children living spaces that, within ever tenacious national and identity-forging traditions, will respect the strangeness of each person within a lay community. Women have the luck and the responsibility of being boundary-subjects: body and thought, biology and language, personal identity and dissemination during childhood, origin and judgment, nation and world—more dramatically so than men. It is not easy to avoid the snares of that condition, which could condemn us exclusively, through regression or flight from the superego, to one side or the other (nationalist or world-oriented militants). (*Nations without Nationalism*, 35)

Reading Campbell, de Jesus, and Chungara together creates a spectrum of reactions to the status of the woman in the nation. Campbell encounters nothing but snares and restrictions, as if enacting Kandiyoti's negative assessment. We might simply say of Campbell that her inability to see beyond the inadequacies of the state to imagine a national community that includes women is a third snare—lonely desperation. Due in large measure to their status as mothers, Chungara and, to a lesser extent, de Jesus demonstrate the ability of women to create their own relationship to the nation and to participate as citizens. However, to participate in their nations, both women must confront at some level the expectation that they have no role beyond the production of future citizens. With regard to these three women, we would do well to remember the frequent association of the modern nation-state with an oppressive patriarchy and to bear in mind that a community imagined as if it were homogeneous often ignores gender inequity in the interest of promoting a masculine national project. As Sylvia Walby has said, "different genders (and classes) may . . . be differentially enthusiastic about 'the' ostensible ethnic/national project, depending upon the extent to which they agree with the priorities of 'their' political 'leaders'" ("Woman and Nation," 84). Furthermore, to again cite Kandiyoti,

> The very language of nationalism singles women out as the symbolic
> repository of group identity. As Anderson points out, nationalism de-
> scribes its object using either the vocabulary of kinship (motherland,
> *patria*) or home (*Heimat*), in order to denote something to which one
> is "naturally" tied. Nationness is thus equated with gender, parentage,
> skin-colour—all those things that are not chosen and which, by virtue
> of their inevitability, elicit selfless attachment and sacrifice. The associ-
> ation of women with the private domain reinforces the merging of the
> nation/community with the selfless mother/devout wife; the obvious
> response of coming to her defense and even dying for her is automati-
> cally triggered. ("Identity and Discontents," 434)

The struggle to move from a "natural" symbolic and maternal position
within the nation to a new and active position within the state, maternal
or not, characterizes the creation of autobiographical identity in these
three narratives.

The state destroys hope and the nation inspires no love in Maria Campbell's *Halfbreed* (*HB*; 1973). Campbell, a Métis or "halfbreed" woman
from Saskatchewan, describes the tense relations between the Indian and
white populations of Canada, stating at one point that she writes her narrative to "tell you what it is like to be a Halfbreed woman in our country" (*HB*, 8). Although Canada represents for Campbell—and, by extension, all Métis women—little more than a displacing power and a
heartless system, she claims it for herself and for other Métis, calling
Canada "our country."[1] However, this early emphasis on group identity
fades quickly, and the hollowness of Métis and Canadian identity in this
narrative soon becomes apparent. Despite Helen M. Buss's contention that
Halfbreed presents a "mapping of self and other that voices not an individual alone, but a community" (*Mapping Ourselves*, 138), group identity appears only weakly in the text. This isolated and angry woman portrays her people as victims of the Canadian state, but she also presents
herself as unable to associate comfortably with the Métis. As Bataille and
Sands observe, "although one learns a great deal about the life of Halfbreed women in Canada from Campbell's story, it is the individual story
of her life that is at the center of her narrative. The dramatic moments, the
frustrations, and the fears are clearly hers, and the concern is with her life,
not with the larger group of Indian women who might share similar experiences" (*Indian Women*, 116). Campbell returns ambivalently in the
final paragraph of her narrative to an expression of unity with the Halfbreeds, but she portrays herself for the most part in retreat from the
world, from Canada, and from her people.

While she hesitates to establish an ethnic identity, Campbell does not equivocate in her discussion of Canada, spurning it both as a nation with which she can identify and as a state to which she owes allegiance. Beyond the most obvious complaint of dispossession, Campbell's rejection of Canada has two motivations. First, she rejects the political and bureaucratic system that humiliates and destroys her people. This is true of those who participate in the programs of the state and those who agitate against the state and its policies. The second motivation lies in the exclusion that Campbell experiences due to her poverty and to her racial heritage.

Two incidents from *Halfbreed* illustrate how confrontations with bureaucracy motivate Campbell to reject Canada. During Maria's adolescence, her father becomes involved in an organization dedicated to regaining the land that the Métis need to maintain their way of life, thus creating hope for change and improvement. Maria's father becomes so deeply committed to political activism that the local schoolteacher jokes that "Saskatchewan has a new Riel" (*HB*, 66), referring to Louis Riel, the Métis leader of the Red River insurrection of 1885. Disappointments soon crush the political commitment of Maria's father, and she says:

> It was the first time I'd ever heard my father cry. Mom put her arms around him and held him, while Cheechum [Campbell's great-grandmother] just sat there and said nothing. Finally Daddy said to her, "Grannie, we've failed. We can't do it." I crept back to bed and later, when I heard Cheechum go outside, I followed her. We said nothing for a long time—just sat there beside the slough and listened to the frogs sing. Finally Cheechum put her arms around me, and holding me close, said, "It will come, my girl, someday it will come." She told me that some of the men had been hired by the government, and that this had caused much fighting among our people, and had divided them. (67)

A subsequent comment reinforces the futility of opposing such a powerful enemy: "We never saw any of the men again who had come to lead our people. They had found government jobs and didn't have time for us anymore" (67). In *Halfbreed*, the government always wins.

The degrading influence of welfare continues the depiction of the Canadian state as a hostile power and provides a second motivation for Campbell's rejection of Canada. After living in Vancouver as a drug-addicted prostitute, Campbell decides to seek welfare assistance. A friend advises her to "act ignorant, timid and grateful," saying "they like that" (*HB*, 133). Campbell follows this suggestion and obtains government assistance, but she leaves the social worker's office feeling "more humiliated and dirty and ashamed than [she] had ever felt in [her] life" (133). Speaking as a member of a group that has struggled for years against a society intent on accumulating Métis lands and against a government all too willing to organize that dispossession, Campbell turns to the state for assistance in fear. Furthermore, since she sees the overall economic conditions of her people—described by Sealey and Lussier as "a cesspool of unemployment, social ostracism by Whites, spiritual and physical degradation, hunger, long term malnutrition, disease and squalor" (*Métis*, 145)—as in large part the result of the initiatives, policies, or neglect of the Canadian government, feigning stupidity for a few dollars of assistance is deeply humiliating. Maria's reaction to her experience in the welfare office mirrors the counsel given earlier by her great-grandmother, of which Campbell says:

> My Cheechum used to tell me that when the government gives you something, they take all that you have in return—your pride, your dignity, all the things that make you a living soul. When they are sure they have everything, they give you a blanket to cover your shame. She said that the churches, with their talk about God, the Devil, heaven and hell, and schools that taught children to be ashamed, were all part of that government. When I tried to explain to her that our teacher said governments were made by the people, she told me, "It only looks like that from the outside, my girl." (*HB*, 137)

As indicated in Cheechum's dour observation, the validity of a claim to be a government by the people depends on what the term "the people" means. In *Halfbreed*, Campbell makes it clear that in Canada, much as in the relationship between the Quiché and the Guatemalan state, the concept of "the people" does not include the Métis.

Campbell uses the contemptuous term "Road Allowance people" to express this marginal status of the Métis as they appear in *Halfbreed*. This expression refers to the Halfbreed practice of settling in the space between roads and farms after being forced from their homesteads. Living in the margins between public and private space, the Métis are neither inside nor outside the nation, a condition that is far from accidental. Campbell relates how the Métis, after failing as farmers, are eventually forced from their settlements and into the space for which they are named. "Gradually the homesteads were reclaimed by the authorities and offered to the immigrants. The Halfbreeds then became squatters on their land and were eventually run off by the new owners. One by one they drifted back to the road lines and crown lands where they built cabins and barns and from then on were known as 'Road Allowance people'" (*HB*, 13). Here, as elsewhere, poverty and dispossession function as signs of difference.

Much as the name "Road Allowance people" marks the Métis as people who live where "normal" people do not live, diet also serves as evidence of abnormality. In and of itself, the fact that Maria and her siblings eat gophers has no meaning. It is the way that the gopher illustrates difference that makes eating one significant in *Halfbreed*. The Road Allowance people are ashamed and disgusted by their lunches because the gopher becomes a sign of poverty when viewed against apples, cakes, and cookies.

> Lunch hours were really rough when we started school because we had not realized, until then, the difference in our diets. They had white or brown bread, boiled eggs, apples, cakes, cookies, and jars of milk. We were lucky to have these even at Christmas. We took bannock for lunch, spread with lard and filled with wild meat, and if there was no meat we had cold potatoes and salt and pepper, or else whole roasted gophers with sage dressing. No apples or fruit, but if we were lucky there was a jam sandwich for dessert. The first few days the whites were speechless when they saw Alex's children with gophers and the rest of us trading a sandwich, a leg, or dressing. They would tease and call, "gophers, gophers, Road Allowance people eat gophers." (*HB*, 46–47)

The white children are not wealthy; what matters here is difference. While the white children eat foods that are "transparent," normal, or unremarkable in their culture, the Road Allowance children eat foods that mark them as "thick," poor, dirty, and different from the other children.

As a result of this and similar experiences, Campbell views her poverty in national terms. She says at one point, "I used to believe there was no worse sin in this country than to be poor" (*HB*, 56), suggesting that poverty functions like race by moving her people beyond the range within which one can be simply "Canadian." By living in poverty, Campbell transgresses the boundaries of normality, below which the individual becomes different from those "normal" Canadians who need no definition. *Halfbreed* implies, in other words, that the Métis poor function as the "other" of white Canada. From Campbell's perspective, the construction of Canadian national identity relegates her with her people to a powerless and exploited condition, her "difference" from Canada making Canada what it is. As Renato Rosaldo has observed, "full citizens lack culture, and those most culturally endowed lack full citizenship" (*Culture and Truth*, 198). In Canada, omnipresence makes the culture of white children invisible, while the culture of the Métis remains distressingly evident. Consequently, given that power stays in the hands of the white population, the Métis will lack full citizenship as long as their culture marks them as different.

Surprisingly, Campbell does not compensate for this rejection with a strong identification with the Métis, with the Canadian poor, or with women, groups with which she might be expected to enjoy "transparency." Although she makes efforts toward establishing an identity based on a closeness with the Métis and on a political alignment with the underclass, the love/hate relationship between Campbell and the Métis prevents this tentative move from becoming effective. The identity presented in *Halfbreed* is consequently that of an isolated woman, a woman who finds herself "thick" relative to both the Métis and to Canada in general. Significantly, Campbell decides to remain "thick." When Lugones speaks in the passage quoted above of "becoming unaware" of differences to reach "transparency," she identifies the very act that Campbell refuses. Maria Campbell rejects group identity because to accept it would require her to forget her hard-won difference from those whom she finds repulsive.

In other words, Campbell's relationship with "her own" people mirrors the emphasis on differences between white and Métis Canadians that makes her childhood painful. This is true despite expressions of love. For example, while reminiscing about days spent among the Métis, Campbell says, "how I love them and miss them!" (*HB*, 25). She also tentatively identifies herself with the poor (white, native, or Métis) of Canada. Recognizing that the cynicism of the ruling elites—especially those business and civic leaders who know Campbell only as a prostitute—affects an entire class and not just a specific ethnic group, Campbell says: "I realize now that poor people, both white and Native, who are trapped within a certain kind of life, can never look to the business and political leaders of this country for help. Regardless of what they promise, they'll never change things, because they are involved in and perpetuate in private the very things that they condemn in public" (118). However, notwithstanding expressions of love for and loyalty to her people, and despite the implied bond with poor whites, Campbell resists close identification with both groups. Her relations with poor whites form only a minor portion of *Halfbreed*, and she moves to separate herself from the Métis of Canada and, during travels in the United States and Mexico, from all native peoples. I must emphasize that I am dealing only with *Halfbreed*—the material narrated by Maria Campbell in her autobiography. It may well be that editing has distorted a sense of group identity, and it may be that she has become more closely connected with the Métis and with native peoples following the publication of the narrative. This second possibility appears to be the case, given that she is referred to as the "Mother of Us All" by Native American poet and playwright Daniel David Moses (quoted in Bowerbank and Wawia, "Literature and Criticism," 566), and given that Campbell has written several books of children's literature (*Riel's People*, *People of the Buffalo*, and *Little Badger and the Fire Spirit*) in which she portrays native peoples much more positively.

Whatever Campbell's subsequent view, within *Halfbreed* the earliest sign of her discomfort among the Métis appears as a result of the teasing she endures for eating gophers. Understandably upset by the teasing, she does not allow her mother to offer comfort. Rather than accepting consolation, she insists that she hates her parents and all "no-good Halfbreeds" (*HB*, 47). She continues her account of the episode: "When I said the same things to [Daddy] he just sat there while I cried and shouted that the other kids had oranges, apples, cakes, and nice clothes and that all we had were gophers, moose meat, ugly dresses and patchy pants" (47). Maria's great-grandmother takes over at this point, carefully instructing her in the history of the Métis people and more particularly in the danger of division caused by these feelings of difference and inferiority. The great-grandmother whips Maria after the lecture to reinforce the danger of turning against her people, but the willow stick does not create love. Rather than inspiring affection, this episode leads only to increased tolerance for and patience with what Campbell portrays as the failings and general backwardness of the Métis. "My first real lesson had been learnt. I always tried to keep my head up and defend my friends in front of those white kids, even when I knew we were wrong. Sometimes it was very hard to control my disappointment and frustration, and many hours were spent with Cheechum telling her how I felt, and she in turn would try to make me understand" (47–48).

A similar incident concludes very differently. Having told her great-grandmother that she wants to make something of herself and that she does not want to be like the Métis women "who had nothing but kids, black eyes and never enough of anything" (*HB*, 86), Maria is not whipped, but encouraged. This ambivalence—a craving for separation blocked by a duty to unite—is best expressed when, in reference to her people and culture, Campbell says, "I hated all of it as much as I loved it" (102). Whatever lessons she may have learned about the dangers of separating from her people provide only superficial results since Campbell continues to emphasize her difference from them. Consequently, throughout *Half-*

breed "Métis" refers to a group of "different" Canadians—not to an ethnic group championed and defended by the author. Attempts to enforce the ideology of group solidarity through lectures and corporal punishment fail. Far from opening her eyes to the need for unity, the whipping more firmly cements Maria's resistance to identification with the Métis. Coercive means produce the opposite of the desired effect, revealing in the process the ideological or strategic—rather than self-evident, natural, or necessary—quality of group identity.

While it would be unfair to expect Campbell to present her people as unfailingly pleasant or heroic, or her past as an unblemished stretch of happiness, an undeniable sense of distance, hesitation, and even distaste marks her description of the Métis and of her life among them. The accumulated weight of tentative, half-hearted, or qualified expressions of allegiance makes what might have otherwise been a hopeful conclusion sound forced. Campbell gives the impression that she is holding her nose as she advocates unity among the dispossessed of Canada: "one day, very soon, people will set aside their differences and come together as one. Maybe not because we love one another, but because we will need each other to survive" (*HB*, 156).

Whereas *Halfbreed* presents a Canadian woman unable to imagine either a national or an ethnic community without unpleasant and painful associations, *Quarto de despejo: Diário de uma favelada* (*QD*, 1960; which in 1962 was published in English as *Child of the Dark: The Diary of Carolina Maria de Jesus*) portrays a Brazilian woman uncomfortable with her immediate surroundings but committed to the concept of nation. This narrative is remarkable for its strong sense of national identification despite poverty, hunger, and cynicism toward government. Although there are similarities in the experiences of Campbell and de Jesus, the fact that the material conditions de Jesus confronts are more dangerous than those Campbell faces is a key difference. Poverty controls much of the action in *Halfbreed*, but there is no sense that Maria or her children confront life-threatening hunger. *Quarto de despejo* presents a much different world. The urban *favelados* cannot hunt, and starvation is a real threat. Despite differences in the degree to which hunger threatens these women and their families, the lack of food makes motherhood in both cases a more emotionally taxing experience than it would otherwise be. When a hungry child asks for food, de Jesus says, for example, "what a horrible thing it is to see a child eat and ask: 'Is there any more?' These words, 'Is there any more?' ring in the head of the mother who looks in the pot and doesn't have any more" (*QD*, 38).

Carolina Maria de Jesus devotes much of her narrative to descriptions of long days spent gathering scrap paper to sell in order to obtain food for her children. These tedious efforts increase the pain when she tells the children that she has nothing and then watches them—literally—eat garbage. Recognizing the cruelty of the economic and political structures that bind her in poverty, de Jesus closes her diary entry on Abolition Day with the following bitterly ironic observation: "And that is how on May 13, 1958 I fought against today's slavery—hunger!" (*QD*, 29). From the earliest pages forward, she combines the narration of her struggles with an analysis of their causes, identifying the sources of her poverty in the malice of more fortunate Brazilians, in the incompetence of elected officials, and in the immorality of the exploitive economic values that govern capitalism. These forces and behaviors create the *favela* and compel de Jesus to scratch out an existence selling old papers and scrap metal.[2]

Throughout her analysis, de Jesus portrays herself as living on the margins of her society and its economy more explicitly than does Maria Campbell in her narrative. As one result of this marginalization, de Jesus argues that the *favelados* are erased as individuals, recognizing that without the tokens of formal participation in the state, the poor may as well not exist. Speaking of a dead child, she says, "he wasn't carrying any documents. He was buried like any other 'Joe.' Nobody tried to find out who he was. A marginal person doesn't have a name" (*QD*, 41). In the case of this dead child, name carries less weight than the bare fact of death, and death is important only in that it requires someone to see to the burial of the body. In other words, when marginalized people die, they lose whatever minimal meaning they might have had in society. This situation is reversed, however, when living *favelados* seek government aid. As de Jesus learns while seeking assistance, when the poor seek aid, their circumstances do not interest the government, but identifying data do. "That's where I saw tears dropping from the eyes of the poor. How painful it is to see the dramas that are played out there. The irony with which the poor are treated. The only things they want to know are the names and addresses of the poor" (43). Reminiscent of Maria Campbell's humiliating experience in a welfare office, de Jesus leaves a similar office convinced that the government merely tolerates the poor and has no commitment to improve the quality of life in the *favela*.

Similarly, the behavior of more prosperous Brazilians reveals no concern for their poor compatriots. Rather than concern, de Jesus finds cold mockery. This disregard for the hunger in the *favela* is evident in that businessmen prefer to dump food into the river rather than sell it at the low prices the *favelados* could afford. "It was in January when the waters flooded the warehouses and ruined the food. Well done. Rather than sell the things cheaply, they kept them and waited for higher prices. I saw men throw sacks of rice into the river. They threw dried codfish, cheese, and sweets. How I envied the fish who didn't work but lived better than I" (*Child*, 58). In a related scene, a truck arrives in the *favela*, and workers dump cans of food on the ground.

> A truck came to the *favela*. The driver and his helper threw away some cans. It was canned sausage. I thought: this is what those hard-hearted businessmen do. They stay waiting for the prices to go up so they can earn more. And when it rots they throw it to the buzzards and the unhappy *favelados*.
>
> There wasn't any fighting. Even I found it dull. I watched the children open the cans of sausage and exclaim:
> "Ummm! Delicious!"
> Dona Alice gave me one to try, but the can was bulging. It was rotten. (35–36)

The apparent act of charity is actually cruelty. In one case, businessmen dump food into the river to maintain its market value, while in another they toss to the birds and to the *favelados* food that can no longer be exchanged for money. These acts imply that the poor, like the cans of rotten sausage, are essentially worthless, having value only as markers of the lowest extremes of society. This is true on the impersonal level as well as in instances of direct contact. We see this in de Jesus's account of an incident in which a *favelada* begs food from a wealthy woman, only to receive an outrageous insult. "The *favelada* said that the woman of the house came back with a package and gave it to her. She didn't want to open the package near her friends, being afraid that the other women would ask for some of it. She started to think: Is it a piece of cheese? Is it meat? When she got back to her house, the first thing she did was to open the package because, as they say, curiosity is the friend of women. When she unwrapped it, she saw dead rats" (*QD*, 66). The dead rats, like the rotten sausage and the discarded rice, represent the judgment of the poor by Brazilian society. Perhaps because the same system produces the *favela* and wealth, de Jesus believes that outsiders view the *favela* with repugnance. "I feel their hateful stares and I know it is because they don't want the *favela* to be here. They think the *favela* ruined the neighborhood. They are disgusted by our poverty" (60).

The sense of living in the margins beyond "normal" society leads to the development of several metaphors with which de Jesus describes the *favela*. When she says that "the *favela* is a back room and the authorities act like they don't even have such a room" (*QD*, 117), she uses the most common metaphor, but there are many others.[3] De Jesus organizes these images carefully, situating the *favela* at the degraded bottom of a chain of associations. "Eu classifico São Paulo assim," she says, "I classify São Paulo this way: the Governor's Palace is the living room. The mayor's office is the dining room and the city is the garden. And the *favela* is the back yard where they throw the garbage" (31). Dividing São Paulo into regions of varying decency and worth, de Jesus locates the *favela* beyond both respectability and productivity. The fact that businessmen dump rotten goods in the *favela* and that housewives send dead rats there as cynical gifts supports her assessment. From both the outside and the inside, therefore, the *favela* is only a place for refuse—human, commercial, or otherwise. De Jesus cannot always resist the feeling that she belongs in that condition. "At 8:30 that night I was in the *favela* breathing the smell of excrement mixed with the rotten mud. When I am in the city I have the impression that I am in a living room with crystal chandeliers, rugs of velvet, and satin cushions. And when I am in the *favela* I have the impression that I'm a useless object that deserves to be forever in a garbage dump" (36).

De Jesus thus sees herself at times as somehow deserving a life in the *favela*, and the fact that she finds no comfort in the company of those who share her condition increases her grief. Like Maria Campbell, de Jesus feels "thick" relative to the men and women around her. Although she insists on her political alignment with the poor, she cannot translate that sentiment into affection or even respect, perhaps because while she recognizes the revolutionary potential of Brazil's poor, she is disillusioned by what she sees as their vulgarity. She says, for example, "I'm disgusted with what the children see. They hear words of the lowest kind. Oh, if I could just move from here to a more decent area!" (*QD*, 9).

De Jesus takes particular offense when she notes that there is no visible effort toward self-improvement among her neighbors. In contrast to this decay, she presents her efforts to better herself through writing. Speaking of the *faveladas*, she observes, "the thing that bothers me is that the women come to my door to disrupt my precious inner tranquility. But even though they upset me, I write. I know how to dominate my impulses. I only had two years of schooling, but I worked to form my character" (*QD*, 12). Because, in her view, other women are content in their degraded state, de

Jesus prefers solitude to their company. As she says elsewhere, "I like to stay inside the house with the door locked. I don't like to stand around on street corners talking. I like to be alone reading. Or writing!" (22). She is "thick" in the *favela* because she believes, moments of depression notwithstanding, that she does not belong there. As Robert M. Levine notes, "Caroline scorned her fellow *favelados*, reviling them as she fought to elevate her own family from misery" ("Cautionary Tale," 68). This scorn does not go unnoticed by her neighbors, who match her low estimation of them with a keen resentment of her. Carlos Vogt comments on these feelings: "The repudiation by the author of her situation is a visceral one. In the same way and to the same degree she is alienated by it. So much so that her neighbors threw rocks at her on the day that she was to leave the *favela*. The point of estrangement between Carolina and the *favelados* is without doubt the book. Writing it was the way that she found to try to break out of her confinement in the world that she lived in" ("Trabalho," 212; my translation). Whether due to arrogance on the part of de Jesus or to ignorance on the part of her neighbors, the tensions that Vogt describes intensify Carolina's belief that violence and backwardness will destroy her if she does not leave the *favela*.

Given a situation in which government workers and private citizens view the poor with a combination of spite and indifference, and in which the poor are less than united, it comes as no surprise that candidates court the votes of the poor with less than genuine concern for their welfare. Having seen candidates come and go, and recognizing that their promises do not change conditions, de Jesus mocks the entire electoral process, calling it a Trojan horse. Because she has seen smiling politicians come to the *favela* with promises in the past, their apparently benevolent behavior can be dismissed as a transparent ploy. "The politicians only show up here during election campaigns. Senhor Candido Sampaio, when he was city councilman in 1953, spent his Sundays here in the *favela*. He was so nice. He drank our coffee, drinking right out of our cups. He made us laugh with his jokes. He played with our children. He left a good impression here and when he was a candidate for state deputy, he won. But the Chamber of Deputies didn't do one thing for the *favelados*. He doesn't visit us any more" (*Child*, 34). The election of wealthy men who feign love for the poor in order to win their votes does not produce hope for change. This pattern fails because that "love" disappears quickly. Rather than electing those who will only perpetuate the exploitative policies of the state, the poor, according to de Jesus, must represent themselves in order to bring about true change. The hungry poor must assume power in place of ignorant officials with no understanding of the effects of government policy on individual lives. "Brazil needs to be led by a person who has known hunger. Hunger is also a teacher. A person who experiences hunger learns to think about others, and about the children" (*QD*, 27). Although important, the memory of hunger is not enough to qualify one for office, but de Jesus leaves her idea conspicuously incomplete, without elaborating as to how this social transformation should proceed. Nonetheless, her impatience with the *favelados* seems to preempt her participation in a political movement among or for the needy. Despite the potential for betterment through self-representation, her contempt for the poor who surround her blocks hope.

Regardless of the bitterness in de Jesus's assessment of Brazilian society, nation remains an important source of identity. Carolina's "thickness" is for the most part limited to the *favela*, and she suppresses the "thickening" facts of race, class, and gender to imagine herself as a Brazilian rather than isolating herself from the surrounding nation as does Campbell. Notwithstanding the cynicism and spite of her fellow Brazilians, and in the face of government indifference, de Jesus responds to her poverty patriotically, envisioning Brazil as a nation of potential greatness prevented from attaining excellence by the ineptness of the state.

Those passages of *Quarto de despejo* that present de Jesus's patriotism are for the most part moral or emotional observations. The passages motivated by morality express an understandable disappointment with the venality of the nation. For example, her response after reading of a woman who commits suicide does not reveal fear for her own family but anger that such things should happen in Brazil. "It is a national disgrace that someone should kill herself because of hunger" (*QD*, 67). Carolina reacts with a similarly nationally oriented response when an aspiring young man informs her that he is interested only in wealth. "I was horrified. No one has any patriotism any more" (113). The impression produced by these two passages is that of a Brazilian Diogenes wandering São Paulo in a vain search for patriots.

The passages from de Jesus's book that describe nation in terms of emotion are less angry. We read at one point words of pure joy as Carolina admires the world around her: "I contemplated joyously the deep blue sky. I realized that I love my Brazil" (*QD*, 34). This jubilant expression is the least complicated of her declarations of patriotic sentiment, indicating the simple love Carolina feels for her homeland. She later recalls a childhood incident that demonstrates both love of country and a complicated desire to improve it. She relates this fablelike memory:

When I was a little girl, my dream was to be a man to defend Brazil
because I would read the history of Brazil and I knew about war. But
the defenders of the nation were all male. So I would say to my
mother:
  —Why don't you turn me into a man?
  She would say:
  —If you go under the rainbow you will turn into a man.
  Whenever I would see a rainbow I would go running in that direction. But the rainbow was always far from me. Just like the politicians
of our country. I would start to get tired and I would sit down and
cry. But the people must not tire or cry. The people must fight to improve Brazil so that our children won't have to suffer the things that
we are suffering. (56–57)

The belief that she must become a man to participate in history says a
great deal about the young Carolina's sense of gender. The notion that
women are somehow unfit for the kind of patriotic service that de Jesus
suggests supports Kandiyoti's argument, cited earlier, that women are of-
tentimes not "full fledged citizens." In this case, Carolina portrays herself
as a spectator rather than an actor, as a passive observer rather than an
active defender of the nation, as a young girl unable to act as men do: in
sum, as much less than a full-fledged citizen. Equating the always-out-of-
reach rainbow with similarly distant politicians, de Jesus brings this memory into the present and suggests that formal participation in the work-
ings of government grants the kind of "male" power that Carolina lacked
as a girl and continues to lack as a woman. The metaphor concludes with
the contrast between Carolina Maria, who grows tired and cries, and the
people of Brazil who must labor tirelessly in order to bring about a better day for the nation. This contrast implies personal rather than general
pessimism since the people will presumably continue to pursue power even
if a weary Carolina drops out of the race.
    Patriotism dominates this episode. As it stands, the point of the anec-
dote is that all Brazilians should work for the good of Brazil, but Carolina
could well have concluded that under the circumstances, change is impossible and the defense of personal interests is the only rational approach
to life. Her emphasis on Brazil and her duty to improve it indicates the importance that nation has for her. A similar sentiment appears in the final
lines of the narrative in a New Year's Eve prayer, where she asks God to
bless Brazil. Here again, Carolina depicts herself thinking in terms of nation
at a moment when we expect narrower, more personal interests to come

to the fore. Rather than ask for a blessing on her family, Carolina concerns herself with Brazil. In contrast, had Maria Campbell concluded her narrative with a New Year's Eve prayer, a request for a blessing on Canada would have been strikingly incongruent with the rest of the narrative.

The decision that de Jesus makes to present herself as a patriotic Brazilian does not clear her path of obstacles. A nationally based sense of self provides no panacea for those without clearly defined identity, but it does allow this woman a feeling for the scope and the significance of her challenges. Her national aspirations certainly include the hope that a better day for Brazil will mean a better day for herself and for the other *favelados*, but the urgent sense that the nation's failings must be corrected in order to reach any kind of collective morality has as much force as that more personal motivation. By presenting herself as a member of the community of millions of Brazilian citizens, Carolina Maria de Jesus sees her troubles as evidence of a lack of national will for change rather than as indications that she leads a particularly difficult life. When Domitila Barrios de Chungara speaks of the goodness and strength of her people, she creates a similar effect. Her emphasis on shared oppression and on the wisdom of the Bolivian people allows Chungara to present her struggle as evidence of a national predicament. Chungara's narrative, edited by Moema Viezzer and titled *"Si me permiten hablar . . .": Testimonio de Domitila, una mujer de las minas de Bolivia* (*SMPH*, 1977; which was published in English in 1978 as *Let Me Speak! Testimony of Domitila, a Woman of the Bolivian Mines*), resembles *Quarto de despejo* in its implication that the individual suffers because the nation suffers, but it is very different in that Chungara emphatically declares her unity with and affection for the poor in their sorrows and also her solidarity with the downtrodden in their coming political triumph.

Si me permiten hablar demonstrates unity with both local and national groups. Unlike the other two women, Domitila Chungara, who is an activist and a miner's wife from the town of Siglo XX, portrays herself drawing strength from her people and devoting that strength to a struggle to remake Bolivia into a land of freedom and socialist equality. Like Maria Campbell and Carolina Maria de Jesus, Chungara describes relations between poor and wealthy Bolivians in terms of the repulsion inspired by poverty. However, in order to promote national unity, she notes that serious class differences exist and then moves to other issues. Revolution in *Si me permiten hablar* implies the liberation of the international proletariat, but its main meaning lies in a national transformation since revolution will liberate the poor from oppression and more prosperous Bolivians from their "false consciousness." It is true, as Javier C. Sanjinés states, that "Domitila deliberately equates the situation of the narrator with that of the collectivity" ("From Domitila," 139), but we should note that she presents that collectivity in explicitly national, as well as class, terms.

Chungara complicates her concept of nation in an interview given several years after the publication of *Si me permiten hablar*. Responding to a question regarding what concepts guide her thinking on the liberation of Latin America, Chungara states:

> Speaking concretely of Bolivia, I think that we must not forget the different nationalities that exist within our country. . . . We have more than 30 small nationalities in our territory. There are also blacks that were brought from Africa. And there are also, among blacks and among Indians, even if this is what they want to call themselves, those who have enriched themselves by exploiting their brothers. In other words, the society that was brought to us by the Europeans is still alive today. To ignore the fact that in our country there must also be class struggle would be absurd; we have to be realistic. There must be respect for nationalities—for their customs, their culture, their forms of government, everything that goes to make up the idea of nationality —but there must also be class struggle within nationalities, even at the government level. ("Owners," 95)

Class and ethnic nationalism supersede Bolivian nationalism in this passage, reflecting significant changes in Chungara's thinking since the publication of *Si me permiten hablar*. Whereas the earlier text emphasizes national unity across class and ethnic lines, this passage reverses that emphasis. The class, ethnic, and racial differences that are suppressed in *Si me permiten hablar* seem here to have validity simply because they separate. In the context of that kind of political fragmentation, she speaks of "nationalities" rather than "the nation," without the sense of the urgent need to rescue nation from the state that is so prominent throughout her autobiography.

In *Si me permiten hablar*, however, Chungara's rejection of the state controlled by the various presidents, dictators, or strong men discussed in the narrative matches her devotion to nation. Chungara would agree that the state and the nation are two different things, but despite the various massacres perpetrated by the army against the citizens of Siglo XX, and despite the fact that Chungara herself suffers torture, she would object to the idea, put forth by Pierre L. Van den Berghe, that states are simply "killing machines run by the few to steal from the many" ("Modern State," 192). Chungara's critique of the state does not call for the emancipation of the people from state systems but for the replacement of the dependent capitalist state of Bolivia with a socialist state. Her critique emphasizes the need to put an end to political and economic brutality, and she argues repeatedly that socialism alone will cure Bolivia of these ills.

Speaking of the inhumanity of Bolivia's economic practices, Chungara addresses two primary concerns: the "plunder capitalism" that depletes resources and the exploitation of the miners who create the nation's wealth. After discussing Bolivia's economic potential, for example, Chungara expresses her concerns over its problems with two questions: "Now then, if it is true that Bolivia is such a rich country in raw materials, why is it a country with so many poor people? And why is its standard of living so low in comparison with other countries, including those of Latin America?" (*SMPH*, 18). Where, in other words, have the nation's riches gone, and why have those who have ruined their health producing them seen so little of that wealth?

To explain the predicament of her people, Chungara turns first to the "tin barons" who, despite the fact that they are Bolivians, reduce their nation to poverty by exploiting its resources and then investing their profits in foreign economies. The influence of these men—Aramayo, Hochschild, and Patiño—was so great during the early years of the twentieth century that Waltraud Queiser Morales has called the Bolivia of those years their "personal fiefdom" (*Bolivia*, 143). Morales goes on to explain the impact of Bolivia's dependence on those men and on the tin industry:

> Even in its heyday, the tin economy induced a chronic structural
> disease of underdevelopment—declining terms of trade—whereby
> dependence on less-valued exports of primary raw materials gener-
> ated trade earnings insufficient to import expensive manufactures
> and consumer goods. Traditional economic dependence on tin and
> other industrial metals accounted for 97 percent of export earnings
> and 90 percent of fiscal revenues, and most foreign exchange proved
> an intractable problem. Well into the 1990s, Bolivia remained a
> monoproducer virtually hostage to fluctuating world minerals
> prices. (143)

Chungara describes these "barons" as traitors, faulting them less for their greed than for their betrayal of national interests, since through their disloyalty they perpetuate for their own gain the dependency that Bolivia has suffered since the days of the Spanish conquest.

Bolivia's export economy is the root cause of that dependency. Because the amount of money generated through mining depends on world minerals markets, and because that revenue is, for the most part, invested in foreign concerns, with the bourgeoisie retaining the lion's share of the remainder, the workers are not paid as much as they should be. To correct this injustice, Chungara, much like de Jesus regarding Brazil, does not imagine a day when the elected officials of the Bolivian state will more carefully consider the needs of the poor. Rather than waiting for reform or for the election of sympathetic officials, she plans revolutionary changes that will thoroughly transform the state by bringing to power the worker and his or her understanding of economics. She prefaces a discussion of future plans, for example, by saying, "one day we will be in power" (*SMPH*, 31), in full confidence that this day will arrive, and that when it does, the system that directs profits to the government and to capitalists will be replaced with a more equitable structure:

> It's like this: if we were to change this system, if the people were in control, with the means that would be adopted, such things wouldn't happen. Our lives would even be longer. . . . We would buy new machinery, for example, so that the labor would be more efficient. The diet of the miner also has to be more in accordance with the physical exhaustion that our husbands have to endure. Furthermore, I think that our husbands shouldn't have to slowly kill themselves working in the mines. You start working there, and until the day that you can't pick up a shovel or a pick, it's only then that you have the right to retire and receive a little compensation. Before that they don't give you a dime. (*SMPH*, 31)

As a point of principle, Chungara anticipates changes to ensure that those who perform the greatest labor will no longer suffer the greatest privations. Again, the reorganization that she describes is not a rejection of government but a restructuring of government so as to protect rather than exploit citizens. Her assurance that her people have learned from previous mistakes and are rapidly becoming equal to the task of governing buttresses her confidence that revolutionary changes will soon come. To make this point, Chungara refers to the Revolution of 1952, also called the National Revolution.

This revolution, which Herbert S. Klein has called "Latin America's most dynamic social and economic revolution since the Mexican Revolution of 1910" (*Bolivia*, 226), was precipitated by an attempt by the Bolivian army to block the ascension to power of the MNR (National Revolutionary Movement) candidate, Paz Estenssoro. The revolt of the army was blocked by an extraordinary combination of government and popular action. Klein notes: "In three days of intensive fighting, during which the armories were opened to the public and the miners marched on La Paz, the army was finally defeated. At the cost of much destruction and the loss of over 600 lives, the MNR returned to power" (225). Radical changes were quickly enacted, including acts bringing about universal suffrage, a drastic reduction in the army, and sweeping reforms in the nation's mines. Of these changes, the most significant is the nationalization of the mines, in which control of the mines for the most part was placed in the hands of the miners themselves via their leftist leaders. These advances began to disappear with the decision to provide indemnification to the "tin barons" and with reliance on aid from the United States to meet the costs of the dramatic changes brought about by the revolution.

Chungara speaks of the revolution as a genuine victory for the people but also as an opportunity lost by the workers due to their lack of political acumen. It is the surrender to the pressure of the United States and the subsequent economic hardships suffered by the miners that inspire her complaint. In describing that political ignorance and its consequences, she says:

> The Revolution of 1952 was a great event in the history of Bolivia.
> It was a true popular victory. But what happened? It was that the
> people, the working class, the *campesinos*, we weren't prepared to
> take power. So, since we didn't know anything about laws, since we
> didn't know the first thing about running a country, we had to turn to
> the bourgeoisie who claimed to be our friends and in agreement with
> our ideas. We had to give over the government to a doctor, Victor Paz
> Estenssoro and others. But they immediately created a new bourgeoisie,
> making new people rich. And those people started to undo the revolu-
> tion. And we, the workers and *campesinos*, we live in worse condi-
> tions than we did before. (*SMPH*, 53)

As evident in this passage, when Chungara turns to a critique of the political situation of Bolivia, she does not argue for the dismantling of government or for the dissolving of borders. Her primary concern is that the worker learn the details and hard facts of governing in order to prevent the bourgeois usurpation of power in the future.

Given her belief that economic dependence is the primary cause of Bolivia's problems, even the violence used by the government against its own citizens is only a symptom of that most serious failing. Furthermore, since even after the Revolution of 1952 the state soon agreed to meet the demands of foreign powers, Chungara describes Paz Estenssoro, the president brought to power in the revolution, as unwilling to "pay attention to what the people said and wanted," despite the fact that he proclaims himself a "nationalist revolutionary" (*SMPH*, 72). Responding more directly to the dictates of the International Monetary Fund (IMF) than to the desires of the Bolivian people, the party of Paz Estenssoro loses the legitimacy it had enjoyed as the enforcer of the popular will.[4] On the other hand, when General René Barrientos Ortuño later took over in a coup, the workers did not hesitate to identify his government as hostile to their interests: "the people manifested their disagreement with that government that was not elected, that was not going to save Bolivia. And our leaders advised us that things were going to happen against the people. In other words, the people can predict and realize when a government is guided by the people and when it is imposed from above. And if it is imposed from above, we have no confidence in that government" (101).

Nonetheless, even though it sins against the nation by ignoring the needs of its citizens, by its illegality, or, even worse, by submitting to the control of foreign powers, the state merits allegiance as a *Bolivian* government. This point becomes clear in a conversation between Chungara and a CIA agent prior to her torture at the hands of officers of the Bolivian military. The importance of this scene can only be appreciated by recognizing that its date, 17 June 1967, places the conversation less than a year after the takeover by Barrientos. The episode occurs, in other words, under a regime that Chungara vigorously denounces as imposed rather than elected. She reports this conversation as follows:

> Since there was already talk in Siglo XX about the CIA and since I
> had seen in films how the intelligence service operates, I had some
> idea about what was happening.
> —We want to help you. Your children will go abroad to study.
> I asked them what they wanted.
> They told me that they wanted to know who were "involved in the
> guerrilla," where the weapons were, etc., etc.
> That's when I told them:
> —Who are you to ask me that? If I have problems with the syndicate or political problems, that's something that I'll resolve with *my government*. I should be asking you: Who are you? What are you doing here? I am a citizen of Bolivia, not of the United States.
> (*SMPH*, 34; emphasis added)

Chungara's refusal to speak to this agent expresses less a hatred of the United States than an acute sensitivity to the loss of both dignity and sovereignty implied in his presence. Even though she deals here with a government that has seized power illegally and against the will of the people, Chungara, ever the vigilant patriot, decries the crime of allowing foreigners to dictate or carry out policy for Bolivia. After her release from prison, Chungara, aware here as elsewhere that the failings of the state are not necessarily the faults of the nation, takes comfort in her father's words: "One day this government will fall, it won't last forever" (175).

The transience of the state contrasts with what Chungara depicts as the enduring strength of her people—the nation. In the face of even the most grievous assault, the women and men who surround her provide constant guidance, courage, and assistance in the struggle to bring about a free Bolivia. Because she attributes so much of what she becomes to the teaching of others, Chungara directs attention or credit away from herself and toward the group. "I don't want you to interpret the story that I'm going to tell as just a personal problem. Because I think that my life is linked to my people. The things that happened to me could have happened to hundreds of people in my country. I want to make this clear, because I realize that there have been those who have done much more than I have for the people, but who have died or who have not had the chance to be known" (*SMPH*, 13). This recognition of the influence that the community has had in her life does not suggest that Chungara's experiences and responses agree perfectly with those of the group. It is instead an expression of a willingness to suppress difference in the interests of creating "transparency," or unity of vision, in an effort to save the nation. Similarly, in Chungara's assessment of the failure of the Bolivian people to sustain the advances of the Revolution of 1952, she speaks in the humble first person plural rather than in the accusing third person. Including herself among the naive and unprepared even though she was too young to have participated, Chungara shows in this instance that she deliberately *chooses* to foster "transparency." In contrast to Maria Campbell, Chungara willingly effaces herself to better promote the interests of the group. She strategically "becomes unaware" of difference, as Lugones suggests is necessary for "transparency."

By giving credit for success to the people, Chungara continues the emphasis begun in the opening pages of the narrative. Counter to autobiographical conventions, Chungara does not begin her narrative with childhood memories or with a recounting of the circumstances of her birth.

Rather than focusing on herself as an individual, Chungara begins *Si me permiten hablar* with a brief analysis of Bolivian history and politics. The collectivity replaces the self not just as a marker of the generic shift from autobiography to *testimonio* but as an indication that "transparency" relative to the Bolivian nation is much more than an important concern within the narrative. More than a controlling idea, national identity represents the central component of the personal identity created and the political ideology advocated by Domitila Barrios de Chungara. Importantly, this sense of being in and belonging to the nation implies the right and ability to participate in the political process. Although she and her companions in the "The Housewives' Committee of Siglo XX" must confront the sexism of their husbands and fathers, the reluctance of men to listen to women is never treated as anything more than a temporary obstacle. Similarly, Chungara criticizes traditional sex roles for their restricting effect, but she is also quick to emphasize that "women's work" can be a revolutionary service:

> The important thing for us women is the participation of the man and the woman together. It is only in this way that we will bring about a better day, a better people, and greater happiness for everyone. Because if the woman continues to worry only about the home and remains ignorant of other facts of our reality, we will never have citizens capable of leading the country. Because that kind of training begins in the cradle. And if we consider the primary role the woman plays as a mother who must train our future citizens, well then, if she isn't prepared she will raise nothing more than mediocre citizens who will be easily manipulated by the capitalists and by their bosses. But if that mother has been politicized, if she has been trained, she will train her children from the cradle with other ideas and those children will be something very different. (*SMPH*, 43)

Value as a "full-fledged citizen," in other words, includes the woman's ability to participate in public discourse, but it is also a matter of her responsibility to inculcate a liberating, as opposed to alienating or restrictive, ideology in her children. Willy O. Muñoz has noted of *Si me permiten hablar*, "within this revolutionary context, Chungara emphasizes that the class struggle must have priority over gender inequalities" ("Conciencia," 74; my translation); and this comprehensive view of the struggle means that traditional household duties should be undertaken with the transformation of society in mind.

Since nation has a central place in her sense of self, Chungara will not allow others to define nation in ways that demean or exclude women or the poor. While jingoistic diversions distract bourgeois nationalism from more essential tasks, she advances a patriotism that defines the nation from the bottom up. The Chaco War (1932–35), for example, was begun by President Salamanca in an effort to gain power over land controlled by Paraguay and Brazil that was thought to hold significant oil deposits. In military and economic terms the war was an unqualified disaster, with tens of thousands dying on the Bolivian and Paraguayan sides of the conflict. However, as Waltraud Queiser Morales points out, the war did serve the ends of the nationalists since a coherent sense of Bolivian nationality grew as a result of the war:

> The Chaco War was perceived as a means to achieve Bolivian na-
> tional, ethnic, and moral regeneration. And, in a manner opposite
> from what had been intended, the war did serve that end. . . . for the
> Hispanic whites life in the trenches in close daily proximity with the
> long-suffering Indian often compelled a grudging compassion, under-
> standing and respect. In many ways defeat in the Chaco shattered old
> racial prejudices; it made possible the acceptance of a national iden-
> tity that became coterminous with ethnic heterogeneity and cultural
> autonomy and the basis for the new era of multi-racial and multi-
> class politics. ("National Identity," 50–51)

Given the failed effort to gain territory in the Chaco War, it is fasci-
nating to note that Chungara thinks in terms of territory when she speaks of the nation. She comments at one point that Chile has stolen Bolivia's access to the sea (*SMPH*, 44), referring to territory lost to Chile in 1879 during the War of the Pacific. Chungara is careful to state that her people harbor no ill will toward the people of Chile, but the fact that she men-
tions the issue is telling. Her concept of nation is based primarily in her notion of a unified people, but we see in the reference to Chile that she also imagines Bolivia geographically—including territory lost nearly one hundred years earlier.

Chungara's comments on the territory of the nation are interesting because they are rare. The bulk of her concern is with the formation of cit-
izens and with the creation of national unity in intellectual and economic terms. In the following passage she explains the role of official education in the development of those goals:

I believe that education in Bolivia, despite various reforms, is still subject to the capitalist system that we live in. They still give us an education that alienates us from the truth. For example, the fatherland, they
teach us to see it as a very beautiful thing that exists in the national
anthem, in the colors of the flag, and in all those things that don't
make sense when things aren't right in the country. The country, for
me, is everywhere, it is in the miners, in the *campesinos*, in poverty, in
nakedness, in malnutrition, in the sorrows and joys of our people.
This is the nation, do you see? But in the schools they teach us to sing
the national anthem, to march in parades and they tell us that if we
refuse to march that we aren't patriots, and nonetheless, they never
tell us the reasons for our poverty, the cause of our misery, the reasons
for the situation of our parents who sacrifice so much without being
paid adequately, the reason why some children have everything and so
many others have nothing. They've never explained this to me in the
schools. (*SMPH*, 60)

The state allegiance promoted by teachers and visible in ritualistic expressions such as saluting the flag or singing the national anthem appears
hopelessly superficial when compared with Chungara's humanitarian nationalist devotion. The symbols and rites of citizenship are literally worthless for her as long as the poor and the hungry are ignored. Whereas the
state overlooks inequity to teach an abstract patriotism, the poor orient
and focus Chungara's patriotism. Imagined in this way, nation allows all—
poor and wealthy, men and women—to participate fully since none are
forgotten, forced to live at the margins of society, or required by difference to exist merely as the defining "other" of full citizens.

Responding to the violence of the state by including all Bolivians in her
concept of nation, Chungara creates an identity designed to foster and emphasize both local and national "transparency." By portraying herself as
the beneficiary of the wisdom and strength of her people rather than as an
isolated sufferer, she looks past the failings of the state in anticipation of
a liberating revolution. Carolina Maria de Jesus and Maria Campbell, on
the other hand, do not present themselves in these terms. Since they portray themselves as "thick" locally, their hopes for the future are limited to
lonely prayers for God's blessing on Brazil or to a qualified anticipation
of a day of unity for Canada.

By forcing them to the margins of their respective communities, social
restrictions and physical dangers compel these three women to react to nation and to state as they form identity. Marginalized, deprived, or physi-

cally violated by hostile powers, these women respond to the state and to the nation by emphasizing either their exclusion from or participation in them. Of the three writers, the only participant in a viable political movement, Domitila Barrios de Chungara, unlike Maria Campbell and Carolina Maria de Jesus, can strategically present herself and her people in terms of mutual dependence, unity, and love of nation. This portrayal allows her to participate as a full-fledged citizen, confident that the wisdom and goodness of her people will bring about a brighter future for her nation. While it is true that her circumstances determine who she is by inspiring opposition, her response to brutality provides evidence that for all its intimidating power, an oppressive state need not limit the individual woman to retreat, despair, or estrangement from nation. To return to Kristeva, the three women considered here all have the "luck and responsibility of being boundary-subjects." Only Chungara is able to turn that condition "through lucidity rather than fate" into one of power and hope. As we see in the next chapter, the strategic quality of her Marxist patriotism links her efforts to those of Omar Cabezas and Pierre Vallières.

3

Myths of Revolution and Nation in Pierre Vallières and Omar Cabezas

Si me permiten hablar shows that Domitila Chungara's love of nation is nuanced and given political "teeth" by Marxism, but her patriotism precedes theory. The opposite appears to be true for the Québécois Pierre Vallières and the Nicaraguan Omar Cabezas. Chungara begins and ends with love of country, whereas these men discover or recognize the strategic value of nation in the course of making their revolutions. A further difference between Chungara and these men lies in their efforts to either debunk or inflate a mythic national essence as a major part of their political programs.

When Anthony Smith notes "the problem of deciding who shall count as 'the people,'" (*Nations and Nationalism*, 148), he articulates an issue of central importance for all the autobiographers whom I study here, but of particular significance for Vallières and Cabezas. These two men are more aggressive than the other authors about defining and delimiting their nations, and they build those definitions through and against myth. This effort places myth at the heart of Vallières's *Nègres blancs d'Amérique: Autobiographie précoce d'un "terroriste" québécois* (1968; which was published in Engish in 1971 as *White Niggers of America: The Precocious Autobiography of a Quebec "Terrorist"* [WN]) and Cabezas's *La mon-*

taña es algo más que una inmensa estepa verde (*LMEAM*, 1982; which was published in English in 1986 as *Fire from the Mountain: The Making of a Sandinista*).

As demonstrated in chapter 2, Chungara emphasizes national affairs by stressing the shared nature of her strength and her suffering. Insistent throughout her narrative that *Si me permiten hablar* is "not just a personal story" but a record of the problems that afflict an entire people, Chungara effaces herself to better present and promote national unity against the evils of foreign domination and the venality of men like the "tin barons." Chungara insists that Bolivia will be free only when it becomes a socialist country, reminding her reader that this *testimonio* is designed more to persuade her compatriots of the need for revolution than to inform foreigners of conditions in Bolivia. The belief that only socialism can liberate Bolivia includes two key points that effectively abstract the argument of Chungara's narrative: socialism is the only system capable of ending the dependency and oppression of Bolivia, and the release from foreign domination will be a specifically national liberation.

Reflecting concerns of Marxist national liberation movements the world over, *Si me permiten hablar* includes a recognition of the international nature of the struggle against imperialism. Chungara says, for example: "And we are not alone. How many peoples are in the same struggle! And why not say it? Every people needs the solidarity of others, because our fight is a great one. So, we have to practice the proletarian internationalism that many men and countries have proclaimed, because, just like Bolivia, many other countries suffer persecutions, abuses, murders, massacres. And how wonderful it is to feel that in other countries we have brothers who support us, that are united with us, who make us see that our battles are not isolated!" (*SMPH*, 44).

Chungara's struggle, therefore, is twofold, with an awareness of the global scope of the war against imperialism moderating her national focus. The duality of this struggle ties it to the tension in Marxist theory between the demands of the particular national situation and the need to defeat international imperialism. The details of the arguments involved are beyond the scope of this study, but the importance of those issues is made clear in S. Neil MacFarlane's assessment of the tensions between international and national orientation in Marxist thought. MacFarlane observes that this tension has been great enough to affect "the whole gamut of issues relating to Third World revolution: the objectives of national liberation, the place of the national liberation movements in the 'world revolutionary process,' nationalism, the adjustment of theory to local conditions . . . leadership, membership, and class relations within the national liberation movement . . . and the use of force in struggles for liberation" (*Superpower Rivalry*, 25). Recognizing the complex issues involved in the local and the international applications of Marxism, Chungara insists that theory conform to her national situation instead of expecting a generic Marxism to provide a valid analysis of and remedy for Bolivian problems. She states to this effect, "Marxism, as I understand it, should be applied to the reality of each country" (*SMPH*, 256). A similar tension between local application and global theory is at work in the autobiographies of Vallières and Cabezas. The two texts are explicitly Marxist in their orientation, but the authors use the concept of nation in radically different ways. Despite the differences, nation is in both cases presented through myth.

When used positively in *Nègres blancs d'Amérique* and *La montaña es algo más*, "myth" corresponds to a definition of the term as narratives or codes whose ideological function is to instill in the citizens of a state or in the members of a group a sense of shared history, destiny, and revolutionary potential. As Terry Eagleton says, "oppressed groups tell themselves epic narratives of their history, celebrate their solidarity in song and ritual, fashion collective symbols of their common endeavour" (*Ideology*, 190), which produce the collective identity necessary for mass action. This is the positive sense of myth for these narratives, by which I mean the sense of myth used by Vallières and Cabezas as a tool to inspire and motivate collective political action. In its negative connotations, as in Vallières's critique of Québec, myth is a code that justifies and perpetuates a senselessly oppressive way of life. This seems to be what Eagleton has in mind when he notes that the disadvantaged "may perceive that their conditions leave a lot to be desired, but rationalize this fact on the grounds that they deserve to suffer, or that it is somehow inevitable, or that the alternative might be a good deal worse" (52). Vallières energetically criticizes this kind of myth as he finds it built up around Québec, and he attributes the failings of the Québécois to what he sees as that self-damning sense of self.

By speaking of national myths, in other words, I do not suggest that these narratives are etiological accounts of the beginnings of Québec or of Nicaragua. These are not the "myths of common descent" that figure prominently in Walker Connor's definition of nation when he says, "in its pristine meaning, a nation is a group of people whose members believe they are ancestrally related. It is the largest group to share such a myth of common descent; it is, in a sentient sense, the fully extended family" ("Nation and Myth," 48; emphasis added). This definition is useful as an aid in understanding "nation" in general terms. It is most helpful here, however, for the contrast it provides since neither Québec nor Nicaragua is presented as a homogenous nation by Vallières or Cabezas. Ethnicity is a central factor in Québécois identity, but not in the sense that would suggest that all French Canadians descend (or believe that they descend) from a common ancestor. Similarly, given the racial and ethnic mixture characteristic of Latin America, it would be odd to think of Nicaraguan nationalism in terms of common and exclusive descent.

In the contexts of Québec and Nicaragua as Vallières and Cabezas present them, "national myth" refers to the group identity derived from a sense of shared and more or less recent history rather than from a "sense of shared blood" extending backward into the primeval ages. To further define Vallières and Cabezas, we might say that Pierre Vallières is what John Hutchinson calls a "political nationalist," a man whose primary goal vis-à-vis the nation is to "secure a representative state for [his] community so that it might participate as an equal in the developing cosmopolitan rationalist civilization" (*Dynamics*, 122). Hutchinson would call Omar Cabezas, by contrast, a "cultural nationalist" who sees the essence of Nicaragua as "the product of its unique history, culture and geographical profile" (122). Cabezas differs sharply from Hutchinson's definition, however, in that he presents the Sandinista state as the purest expression of the national essence rather than as an accidental addendum to the nation.

Defined ethnically, historically, or in terms of an affiliation with a political program, the nation and its myths are tied to revolution throughout *La montaña es algo más* and *Nègres blancs d'Amérique*. More specifically, the use of national myths constitutes a direct appeal to popular sentiment in the efforts of Vallières and Cabezas to equate the essence of Québec and Nicaragua with their political parties: for Vallières, the Front de Libération du Québec (FLQ), and for Cabezas, the Frente Sandinista de Liberación Nacional (FSLN). In the case of Vallières's analysis of nation, myths that justify the continuing isolation of the Québécois are discarded as counterproductive and are replaced by a Marxist mythology through which he seeks to explain current conditions and, ultimately, to transform society. Omar Cabezas, on the other hand, exploits myths of the Nicaraguan national essence as an outlet for the new sense of personal identity that follows his experiences as a *guerrillero*, but also to depict the FSLN as the embodiment of the united popular will. Like Chungara, these men include a global element in their narratives, but the importance of internationalism varies greatly from text to text. For Cabezas, the national essence is primary, with global concerns appearing in a subordinate role. Vallières, on the other hand, addresses national concerns impatiently, since his first concern is world revolution.

It is the power of myth to obscure the realities of economic oppression and cultural stagnation that most provokes Vallières. *Nègres blancs d'Amérique* interweaves a narration of his experiences with a presentation of his dream of "total revolution" for a Québec trapped in an ideological system that sustains inequity, ignorance, and misery. The circumstances surrounding the writing of *Nègres blancs d'Amérique* merit brief mention here, as those harsh conditions may in part explain Vallières's impatience with mythic and otherwise immaterial descriptions of society. Written while Vallières was imprisoned in a New York City jail for protesting in front of the United Nations building, the book is presented not as a polished piece of writing but as a political act. Vallières states in his foreword, "the book was written in prison, immediately after a twenty-nine day hunger strike, under particularly difficult conditions. It was written in the midst of the constant noise of cells being opened and closed by an iron hand and of guards shouting back and forth, and within the framework of an absurd discipline (called prison rules), invented and applied for the purpose of brutalizing the inmates as much as possible" (*WN*, 9). Given these circumstances, the recurrent bitterness and occasional venom of a book that Malcolm Reid praises for its "unliterary, unembellished, unsubtle, uncouth—but not illiterate" quality is not surprising (*Shouting Signpainters*, 281).

Although the book was written at a time of personal suffering, Vallières is more concerned with the condition of a people than of a person, presenting extended commentary on the social and economic condition of Québec and on the ways that the Québécois have been dominated by the French, the British, and the Americans. Interestingly, his first concern is not with imperialism. As serious as foreign imperialism is, he places the blame for the economic woes of Québec squarely on the Québécois themselves. Vallières's anger grows as the narrative progresses through descriptions of what he sees as a self-inflicted oppression perpetuated by mythic rather than material definitions of self. In his view, there is only one valid approach to the problems of the Québécois, and that approach is material. "The heart of the problem," he says, "is neither metaphysical nor moral. It is material, it is at the same time economic, historical, and military. Consequently its solution must be of the same nature. Since the evolution of humanity is not a philosophical system, there is no theoretical solution to the problems it raises. There are only practical solutions" (*WN*, 56). Much as Chungara maintains that the nation is composed of the hunger and the poverty of the people rather than of flags and parades, Vallières insists that the national problem is not so much a matter of identity as it is of exploitation through identity. It is, in other words, a question of what material disadvantages will follow or what material benefits will be produced through a group's definition of itself. Given this approach, mere independence matters very little. As long as the resources of Québec are controlled by foreign corporations, there can be no meaningful change. As he observes, "imperialism is not interested in flags: one flag more or less in no way disturbs its universal system of exploitation of resources and cheap labor" (61). The problems of the French Canadians, in other words, are only prolonged by definitions that describe them in terms of a unique and mythic national essence rather than in terms of material realities shared by exploited peoples the world over.

Those material realities dominate Vallières's description of his early life. He grows up during the years after the transition from an essentially feudal society to an industrial system, at a time when Duplessis, the premier of Québec, allowed foreign capitalists to dominate the Québécois economy. As an example of this foreign control, Vallières cites the exploitation of resources by Americans, which brought sad consequences for the Québécois. "The Americans were making billions off of *our* iron, Duplessis was making millions off the Americans, the political machine of the National Union Party was distributing its millions to the supporters and thugs of the regime . . . and we, poor starving wretches, we had to buy water!" (*WN*, 113). The years of Vallières's youth correspond approximately to the years of the "Quiet Revolution," which was a period during which attempts were made to restructure Québécois society so as to eliminate the inequities that Vallières describes. Jean-Claude Robert describes this period in terms of its nationalist focus: "'Quiet Revolution' refers to the collective transformations experienced by Québec roughly from 1960 to 1966. We note immediately the strictly Québécois character of the period. . . . After 1960, the expression 'French Canadian' reflects less and less the feeling of belonging by citizens of the province who no longer refer to themselves as French Canadians but as Québécois" (*Canada français*, 200; my translation). Regarding these changes as anything but revolutionary, Vallières devotes his life to the fundamental transformation of society through Marxist revolution. He says of this period: "the 'Quiet Revolution' had nothing to say to me. I did not yet perceive any profound change in my country, but only a superficial unrest that was almost all talk" (*WN*, 199). In that economy, the participation of Québécois like Vallières and his father was limited to providing the cheap labor that made large profits possible for those capitalists. Gagnon and Montcalm describe the results of this economic aggression, observing that in the 1960s

"French Canadians controlled a mere 15 percent of the manufacturing industry in the province, and . . . French Canadian enterprises were concentrated in the traditional, low-productivity, labour intensive sectors such as leather manufacturing and woodcutting" (*Quebec*, 25).

However, it is not poverty, underemployment, or exclusion from economic power that concerns Vallières so much as it is the mythic overlay that produces from these conditions what he calls a "manipulated, despised, worn out, powerless, demoralized people" (*WN*, 114). It is not poverty, in other words, that is shameful, but the perpetuation of an ideology that excuses and justifies that poverty. Vallières's argument is that Québécois Catholicism demeans its adherents by ensuring the continuation of their dependent condition. This is brought about as members of the clergy subordinate the interests of the *habitants*, the French Canadians, to the interests of the church through collusion with business interests and, more importantly, through the exhortation to patient suffering of the troubles created by their partnership with mammon. At the personal level, Vallières rejects the ideology of the church by seeking a new life in intellectual pursuits. On the national level, he attempts to repeat this rejection through *Nègres blancs d'Amérique*, which is intended to awaken the Québécois to the ironic fact that their identity as, among other things, *rural, catholique, et français* is a source of economic oppression and cultural isolation. He contends, in other words, that Québécois national identity is not an essence that must be rescued from English Canada, but an avenue through which imperialism has bought up Québec and marginalized the Québécois.

Before the French Canadians could think of themselves as a people rather than as mere expatriate subjects of the French crown, they needed a defining "other." Speaking of the years of transition from French to English rule, Vallières explains how nationalist ideology answered this need by transforming an impoverished group of immigrants into a Catholic (but still indigent) nation positioned against the English and endowed with a redeeming mission.

> Nothing changed in the frugal and monotonous life of the Habitants. They were still beasts of burden, despised in a hostile country. But, God be praised, the clergy received the order from Heaven to make this resigned and silent collectivity into a nation dedicated to the Church. At last the life of slavery would take on meaning by becoming redemption. This people, planted in America by an accident of history, suddenly found itself invested with a supernatural vocation.

Its task, in the pagan world of the savages and the English, would be to save souls by patiently bearing poverty, hard labor, and isolation. The clergy organized the embryonic nation into parishes, created elementary schools and *collèges*, arrogated to itself the right to regulate the lives of individuals and groups, and defined the ideology which was to fashion a vision of the world consistent with the interests of the Church. (*WN*, 25–26)

In ways reminiscent of the strategies of Rigoberta Menchú, the Québécois church responds to aggression by inventing a new identity. Hubert Guindon observes that "as custodian of the nation . . . the Church managed to instil a pride in one's difference and distinctiveness, a passion to survive as a people, an attachment to language and culture in spite of economic poverty, and a deep commitment to traditional Catholicism" (*Quebec Society*, 108). There is little to criticize in the decision, as a kind of survival mechanism, to transform an isolation produced by the hostility of others into a sense of "pride in one's difference" or of cultural mission. Recognizing this, Vallières criticizes the specific form that French Canadian identity takes rather than the will to survive as a distinct group. However, by seizing on every opportunity to emphasize what he sees as the sinister role played by the clergy in this process, he presents what is ultimately an overly simple account. It is, of course, perception that matters in autobiography, but John A. Dickinson and Brian Young present a much less derisive view of the role of the Québécois clergy. Describing a church that would have been in decline in the years of Vallières's youth, they note that the "power, influence, and numerical strength of the Roman Catholic church peaked in the 1950s," that it was "never monolithic," and that as early as the 1940s a Bishop Phillipe-Sevule Danserleau had declared that "capitalism is the cause of all our hurt. We have to work against it, not to transform it—since it is incorrigible—but to replace it" (*Short History*, 285).

As part of his long-running and perhaps unfair reproach of the church, Vallières implies that at the direction of a corrupt clergy, the Québécois have been restricted in the way that they think of themselves—in the terms of this study, that they have been restricted in the ways that they imagine their community. He faults the way the Québécois have embraced hostile definitions or cruel conditions such as the poverty, hard labor, and isolation mentioned in the passage above as points of identity. Simply setting themselves up, in other words, as whatever the English are not guarantees economic depravation by locking the Québécois out of full participation in the Canadian economy.

Rural rather than urban, Catholic rather than Protestant, and speaking French rather than English, the Québécois position themselves as if to shadow the English as their righteous "other." With the Québécois already cut off culturally through language, their clergy initiate a doomed colonization effort to permit them to develop as a separate people. Although choosing to be rural, Catholic, and French might have been beneficial elsewhere, this policy can lead to only poverty and backwardness for the Québécois because, as Vallières points out with characteristic rancor, the land chosen for the project was entirely unsuitable. Separation may well be a fine idea, in other words, but the success of such an idea must be measured materially. It simply will not do, in Vallières's strictly materialist thinking, to gauge the achievement of a people in terms of their faith or devotion to God—all the more so when those beliefs explain away and even increase poverty. Against a history marked by recourse to a mythic sense of cultural being, the force of Vallières's argument is that Québec cannot be free until it throws off Catholicism. To begin this process, he urges the total separation of the Québécois and their myths by leading a rhetorical charge against their patron saint. "Let us kill Saint John the Baptist! Let us burn the papier-mâché traditions with which they have tried to build a myth around our slavery" (*WN*, 20).

This assault on the spiritual foundations of the Québécois nation does not necessarily indicate a hostility toward religion per se. Vallières distinguishes his argument from a general attack on faith by saying: "I have nothing against those who believe in God. But I do have something against those who believe they are exempt from opposing injustice and taking practical action against it, those who believe they are justified in remaining neutral by virtue of imaginary divine commandments" (*WN*, 157). Although this distinction between a sincere belief in God and a religion that simply provides cover for cowardice or passivity is a fairly careful one, and as helpful as it is in explaining Vallières's recurring interest in religion, the circumspection is ultimately beside the point.[1] The proposition of the symbolic murder of a central cultural figure is an act of violence against Québec that prefigures a complete break with it.

It comes as no surprise, therefore, that after disappointments in love and a deeply disillusioning period spent writing for journals such as Pierre Trudeau's *Cité Libre*, Vallières is ready to leave his homeland for good. The need to find a people with the courage to act on his revolutionary principles partially motivates his departure for France, but the journey is as much about getting out of Québec as anything else. Portraying himself sailing away from Québec, Vallières writes himself into a problem. He has dismissed the Québécois as hopelessly deluded, derided their religion, mocked their mythic sense of a heroic past, and then turned his back on them. However, notwithstanding these efforts to undo his sense of national belonging, Vallières must return to Québec—if only because the subtitle of his autobiography describes a specifically national persona: *Autobiographie précoce d'un "terroriste" québécois*. The question is not if he will rescue nation from the ruin he has made of it, but how.

The answer involves the conflict between the international and national applications of Marxism. Vallières experiences a type of conversion in France, but only after spending several months working as a farm laborer and after concluding that the Communist Party in France was more interested in maintaining its power within the existing system than in true revolution. Vallières's transformation is an awakening to the power of Marxism to revolutionize society and to the conviction that real change is within the reach of the workers of the world. Prior to this moment of clarity, Vallières's thinking had been an amorphous mix of contemporary philosophy dominated by existentialism. Marxism, which was previously important but not central, becomes through this experience the lens that focuses his thinking and action throughout the remainder of the narrative.

Despite Vallières's new confidence that change will one day arrive, the tone of his autobiography does not switch immediately from criticism to optimism. Although Marxism brings the possibility of future improvement, it increases his despair in the short term. Disgusted with the pettiness of French communism and convinced that he was of little use to anyone in France, Algeria, Québec, or anywhere else, Vallières considers suicide. This bleak period ends when Vallières is advised that he will never be happy or useful until he returns to his home. A friend, Françoise, tells him, "you have to learn to live with what you are, in your country as it is, neither better nor worse than the others. I am convinced that if you succeed in doing something for your own people, in fighting for them and with them, your life will be completely transformed" (*WN*, 264). Because nationality, according to Françoise, is completely natural, it determines who Vallières is, but it is also only through nation that his idealism can assume authentic and effective form. Nonetheless, despite the encouragement of this friend, Vallières portrays the journey to Québec bleakly, describing himself boarding a train for home "the way one gets into a hearse" (264). Notwithstanding the distaste evident in a further observation that mocks the process of creating national identity that we have seen in Menchú and Chungara, it is at the level of the nation that Vallières must make his contribution to world revolution. He says, "seen from Paris,

Québec looked like a ridiculous provincial town whose inhabitants were turned toward a past they had built into a myth and who had invented a heroic history for themselves out of the meager material available" (264). Like Maria Campbell, this revolutionary goes home holding his nose.

If the remainder of *Nègres blancs d'Amérique* were to detail a genuine resolution of the differences that separate Québec and Vallières, his expressions of disgust for his country could be read as mere drama. However, rather than reconciling himself with Québec, Vallières evades its realities to better portray a community imagined as being on its way to revolution. Given that his reconciliation has more to do with political expedience than with a sense of belonging, his expressions of distaste for Québec highlight the forced or strategic nature of his nationalist sentiment. Interestingly, to make his reconciliation he takes the same step that he condemns the Québécois for taking—he imagines his community in his own less than material terms. Vallières returns, in other words, to a very different Québec, but it is not Québec that has changed. He no longer presents French Canada as a pathetic land of illusions because it is now the potential rather than the material Québec that interests him. Much as the Québec criticized earlier was portrayed as less concerned with reality than with the creations of Catholic ideology, this new Québec is more a projection of Marxist ideology than a political entity with material or economic being. The following passage illustrates the selectivity of this imaginative reconciliation: "As I became reconciled with the world and with 'other people,' I became reconciled with the Québécois French nation, not the one that for centuries has been 'blessed' with poverty, ignorance, and religion, but the one that is at last beginning to say 'no' to exploitation, and is trying to emancipate itself completely. What we have been is less important, in my eyes, than what we shall become if we want to" (*WN*, 201). Vallières is reunited with Québec only insofar as he is able to imagine that community as part of a multinational class consciousness that will lead to a global movement toward revolution. The reconciliation, in other words, is with a Québec that may one day come to be rather than with the Québec that is. Furthermore, that future Québec is imagined as part of a multinational class rather than as a culturally distinct people.

In this utopian scheme, nation and national essence are provisional terms, constituting at best intermediate steps in a global revolutionary process. Consequently, Vallières returns to Québec and dedicates himself to the struggle for its freedom, not because there is something transcendent about his relationship to that part of the world, but because as a product of that region and people, it is there that he can best advance revolution. Similarly, Québécois identity is useful only as a nationalism that is understood as a prelude to a subsequent supranationalism.

> I am 100 percent Québécois, and it is in Québec first that I want to pursue the struggle against imperialism. It is in Québec that I hope with all my heart to overcome tyranny with my comrades, or else to die with them, weapon in hand.
>
> If I were a citizen of the United States, it is in the United States that I would fight first. Revolution is not impossible anywhere. It is necessary in all countries, including today most of the so-called socialist countries.
>
> It does not matter what country is our "native land." It does not matter what difficulties we are daily confronted with: *our duty as revolutionaries*, wherever we may be, *is to make the revolution*, as Guevara so well reminded us before he was vilely assassinated by the CIA in Bolivia. (*WN*, 278; emphasis in original)

By adopting Che Guevara's counsel to "make the revolution" wherever one might be, Vallières implies that the revolution will be essentially the same the world over. Given this sameness, it does not matter where an individual happens to live. For all the effort to describe Québec in terms that fit his political aspirations, it is of little consequence whether or not Vallières is "100 percent Québecois."

To present himself and his people as united in this revolutionary cause, and to think in terms of having or belonging to a people, Vallières must represent Québec through synecdoche. He makes this clear by stating that his reconciliation is not a wholesale identification with his people but a selective reconciliation with those Québécois trying to *s'émanciper totalement*. Having identified a sympathetic group, Vallières amplifies and projects those individuals as if they were all of Québec. Since it is only by presenting Québec as if all its citizens were as fully committed to revolution as he is that Vallières can speak of a complete reconciliation, there is a kind of rhetorical violence at work here. This is all the more apparent when we remember that he explicitly excludes those Québécois who have not taken up the cause of the revolution. What initially appears to be a return to nation, in other words, is actually careful ideological posturing that leads on one hand to a sense of personal worth via a role in the revolution but on the other hand to a depiction of Québec as an extension of self. This extension is perhaps most evident in the concluding lines of the autobiography. "Hey, Georges! What are you waiting for to make up your mind? And the rest of you, Arthur, Louis, Jules, Ernest? On your feet, lads, and *all together*: to work! We'll have another glass of beer when we've done something besides talking and always putting the blame on other people. Each of us has his little share of responsibility to assume and to turn into action. The sooner we are united, lads, the sooner we will win. We have already wasted too much time in vain recriminations. Now we must go on to action" (*WN*, 281). Coupled with the exclusion of those not inclined to support revolution, this tone of easy familiarity strategically levels differences. It is as if the only problem were delay or laziness, rather than fundamental disagreement over goals, ideology, tactics, or identity.

This leveling of differences is also an erasure of women. Calling his compatriots to action, Vallières rallies *les gars*, making no mention of female participation in the struggle. The case of Françoise, the woman who inspires Vallières's return to Québec, also demonstrates the masculine nature of this text. Beyond her brief presence to encourage Vallières to reconcile himself with his country, she appears only as an erotic object with which Vallières consoles himself. He says of her, "one evening when Marcel [the husband of Françoise] was out, I surprised Françoise in the act of washing herself in the kitchen. She was half naked. I could not resist the desire to go up to her, to pass my hands over her neck, her shoulders, her breasts, her belly. I leaned my head against hers and pressed her body tightly against my own. I was crying" (*WN*, 192).

The contrast between Vallières's sexist presentation of women and the inclusive program of Domitila Chungara is enlightening. Whereas Vallières can assume his full citizenship and his right to participate politically by virtue of being a man, Chungara is compelled to assert her rights and to claim a political voice against "the idea that women shouldn't get involved" (*SMPH*, 79). Countering this traditional thinking, Chungara urges equality as the only way to save the nation. "The important thing for us women is the joint participation of the man and the woman" (43). Vallières's coercive and exclusively male "we," in other words, reveals the ideologically heavy-handed use of nation in *Nègres blancs d'Amérique*.

A similarly intimate tone—and male focus—characterizes Omar Cabezas's *La montaña es algo más*. As critics have observed, this narrative is remarkable for its conversational quality and for the use of idiomatic and peculiarly Nicaraguan Spanish. Shirley Christian notes that the book is one of "the first ever written 'in Nicaraguan'—that is, using the colloquialisms of Nicaraguans instead of the rules of the Spanish Academy" (*Nicaragua*, 292). Speaking to his reader throughout the text as *vos*, a colloquial form of the familiar pronoun *tú*, Cabezas addresses an implied reader who is male, revolutionary, and Nicaraguan. For example, when he speaks of the demands of life as a guerrilla in the mountains, Cabezas says, "with the passage of unforgiving time, merciless time, time that goes on and on without ever changing, you lose everything . . . and you lose your mind. . . . You gradually lose yourself, and you are physically transformed" [Vos te vas perdiendo, tu físico se va transformando] (*LMEAM*, 265). As is the case in the conclusion of *Nègres blancs d'Amérique*, the intimate tone levels the differences between people to create the impression of unanimity. Again using *vos*, Cabezas addresses his reader as a compatriot but also, and much more specifically, as a fellow male Sandinista. There is, in other words, much more at stake than capturing the attention and interest of the reader through this intimate form of address; the tone of the narrative established through the pronoun supports and advances the content of directly ideological claims. For example, Cabezas writes, "defininitivamente, el pueblo y el Frente siempre pensaron igual" [without a doubt, the people and the front [the FSLN] always saw things the same way] (*LMEAM*, 26). To support that claim, Cabezas works throughout his narrative to link Nicaragua to the FSLN in ways that give the Sandinistas unique status as the heirs of Sandino and therefore as the embodiment and guardians of the Nicaraguan national essence.

Speaking of the *testimonio* in terms of genre, John Beverley and Marc Zimmerman acknowledge that "the sense of presence of a real, popular voice in the testimonio is, of course, in part illusory" (*Literature and Politics*, 177). Commenting further on the link between the testimonial subject and the "people," Beverley and Zimmerman insist:

> Testimonio cannot affirm a self-identity that is separate from a group or class situation marked by marginalization, oppression, or struggle. If it does this, it ceases to be testimonio and becomes in effect autobiography, that is, an account of and also a means of access to, middle- or upper-class status, a sort of documentary Horatio Alger story. . . . Even where its subject is a person "of the left," . . . autobiography is an essentially conservative mode in the sense that it implies that individual triumph over circumstances is possible. Autobiography produces in the reader, who in most Latin American contexts is already either middle or upper class or looking to be, the specular effect of confirming and authorizing his and (less so) her situation of relative social privilege. Testimonio, by contrast, always signifies the need for a general social change in which the stability and complacency of the reader's world must be brought into question. (177–78)

This observation appears particularly relevant for Cabezas and Vallières since in both cases the alleged unity of self, people, and circumstance is a primary issue. Beverley and Zimmerman present their argument in ways that assume authenticity. There is no room in their formulation, in other words, for a feigned alignment with the group that an author has decided to call "the people," nor is there allowance for narrative strategies that emphasize oppression, marginalization, and group identity as much to build support for their political programs as to bring into question the "stability and complacency of the reader's world." I argue, on the other hand, that it matters very little whether a text is a *testimonio* or an autobiography because, although the unity with group and class that Beverley and Zimmerman require is almost universally valued, *Nègres blancs d'Amérique* and *La montaña es algo más* show that it is also a strategy whose ideological motivations need to be challenged.

Cabezas and Vallières portray group identity through the nation, and their emphasis on national unity highlights some of the important differences between them. Both men resort to synecdoche to portray their nations as unitedly supporting their ideologies, but whereas Vallières maintains distance from Québec, Cabezas upholds and defends the essence of Nicaragua as an integral part of FSLN ideology. This effort is most visible in the conclusion of the narrative where Cabezas, in a moment of joyous recognition, sees that it is only in Nicaragua and through Sandino that he has personal identity. As Beverley and Zimmerman observe, Cabezas conflates self and nation as he narrates the birth of "a new collective national and personal identity" (*Literature and Politics*, 186).

Another major difference lies in the concern the two men demonstrate for Marxism. Vallières dedicates a substantial portion of his narrative to the presentation of conditions in Québec and to the analysis of those conditions in Marxist terms, but in Cabezas's narrative there is virtually no analysis and only limited references to Marxism. Furthermore, the reader learns a great deal about Vallières at various stages of his life, whereas Cabezas's self-portrait includes only those years of active involvement in some form of resistance. This is probably due to the need for Vallières to present an analysis of Québec compelling enough to convince others of the rightness of the Marxist world view and to the need for Cabezas, on the other hand, to downplay the role of foreign influences in the FSLN. Finally, it is important to note the different stages of the revolutions in Québec and Nicaragua. While Vallières works in the hope that the day of actual revolution will eventually arrive, Cabezas is a veteran of an armed conflict who writes in the aftermath of the Sandinista victory. He is an experienced soldier, but due to his focus on ideological issues, military objectives have only secondary importance in his autobiography.

Cabezas closes his narrative before the armed struggle against Somoza comes to its end. That conclusion arrived on 19 July 1979, as revolutionary forces poured into Managua to celebrate the departure of the hated dictator. Describing this euphoric moment, Miranda and Ratliff state:

> In July 1979 a bright new dawn seemed to have come to Nicaragua, after the decades-long night of Somoza dictatorships, just as Sandinista National Liberation Front (FSLN) founder Carlos Fonseca had said it would. The last Somoza fled to Miami on 17 July and two days later the main body of bearded Sandinista troops entered Managua unchallenged by the few remaining members of the former dictator's National Guard. Clad in dirty olive-green uniforms and black berets, the triumphant Sandinistas rode in trucks or marched through the streets mobbed with jubilant Nicaraguans, many of whom had fought as undisciplined members of the FSLN in the final battles. The broad front strategy, which had pulled all the national forces opposed to Somoza together in a nation-wide alliance, had finally brought the dynasty down. (*Civil War*, 1)

For all its emotional, symbolic, and military value, the occupation of Managua was by no means the end of the struggle for Cabezas and his fellow Sandinistas. As Miranda and Ratliff note, it was not the FSLN alone that entered Managua on that July day but a broad coalition of forces that included the UDEL (Unión Democrática de Liberación), the MDN (Moviemiento Democrático Nicaragüense), and the PSN (Partido Socialista Nicaragüense) in addition to the FSLN, which was itself divided by contention between the Tercerista and Proletario factions. United against the Somoza regime, the various opposition parties had placed their differences aside. After the military victory, however, the serious differences between these parties made an ideological contest inevitable. The FSLN prevailed, but the splits and divisions between parties and within the ruling directorate itself did not vanish. These factional disputes led directly to the Contra War and, with that conflict, to the renewed and increased involvement of the United States in Nicaraguan affairs. There was, given the political rivalries that followed Somoza's departure and the efforts of the U.S.-backed Contras to discredit the Sandinista government, a need to legitimize the FSLN regime and to consolidate its political and military control of Nicaragua. *La montaña es algo más* participates in this ideological task by attempting to naturalize the rule of the FSLN. As part of this effort, Cabezas returns to the years before the overthrow of Somoza to link the FSLN's revolutionary campaign to a particular conception of Nicaragua. This is accomplished by connecting the FSLN with Che

Guevara's concept of the *hombre nuevo* (new man) and by equating the Sandinistas with a mythical national essence—Sandinismo. Cabezas does not define the Sandinismo of the FSLN for his readers. There are scattered references to Marxist-Leninist doctrine, but the assumption seems to be either that the reader already knows what Sandinismo is, or that vague notions better serve the cause. As Andrés Pérez notes, this indirect presentation of the guiding ideology of the FSLN is not unique to Cabezas:

> *Sandinismo* never consisted of a coherent set of values and ideas capable of providing FSLN members with the guidelines needed for purposeful action. It was—and still is—a vague, contradictory, and confusing set of nationalistic slogans and proverbs. The principles of non-alignment, political pluralism, and a mixed economy which the *Sandinistas* used to explain and defend their policies and actions contained the seed of a potential, practical *Sandinista* ideology. However, this promise was never realized; these principles were never properly defined, formulated, or developed. On the contrary, they were left open to interpretation in order to ease the accommodation of the various, and contradictory, forces that operated both within the party and the country as a whole. ("FSLN after Debacle," 119–20)

Although Pérez criticizes Sandinismo for what he sees as a suspicious and potentially dangerous lack of definition, it is precisely that openness that Cabezas exploits throughout his narrative. The details of political doctrine are not the stuff of legends; the image and the memory of a heroic freedom fighter, on the other hand, very readily becomes myth, and that myth becomes a myth of national essence in *La montaña es algo más*.

At first glance, a narrative filled with images as concrete and mundane as stealing office supplies, watching a monkey be shot and prepared as a meal, and the details of cleaning a dangerously infected leg might seem to leave little room for myth. This is, Anthony Beevor states, a book whose prose "has an extraordinary intensity of feel and smell as well as sight and sound" ("Last Marine," 14). However, for all the book's gritty realism, it is the mythic imagery that conveys the ideological message of this autobiography. Cabezas depicts his personal growth as a dialectic progression through which the physical and psychic obstacles of mud, exhaustion, and humiliation are overcome as he is transformed into the *hombre nuevo*. Molded in the hands of the FSLN, Cabezas presents himself as both a new man and as the child of a mythic parent—the Nicaraguan patriot Augusto César Sandino.

Since women have no role in Cabezas's mountain setting, he speaks of men giving birth to men. This idea reaches an early high point when, after a long march, Cabezas feels that his training is complete. "We reached the camp and we ate, and then we felt just like veteran guerrillas and they received us just like veterans, and that was just the beginning: we felt like we had birthed ourselves, like everything started right there" (*LMEAM*, 130). The Sandinista soldier gives birth to his new self far from the distractions and the assistance of women. Coquettish nurses, faithless lovers, and sexy *muchachas burguesas* all appear, but when it comes to the *hombre nuevo* that represents the power and goodness of the Sandinista program, there is no room for women in either the process or the product.

As Cabezas indicates, the *hombre nuevo* is best exemplified in the life of Che Guevara. Although important as a revolutionary model for Vallières, Guevara has more of a presence in *La montaña es algo más* than in *Nègres blancs d'Amérique*. Guevara appears most frequently in the phrase *"hay que ser como el Che"* [you have to be like Che], which recalls his example of determination and revolutionary zeal, most particularly during his campaign in Bolivia. Guevara provides a model for both men, but his ideal, the *hombre nuevo*, makes Guevara particularly significant for Cabezas. Donald C. Hodges discusses the Nicaraguan use of the ideal of the new man in his book *Intellectual Foundations of the Nicaraguan Revolution*. Noting that "in Nicaragua the cult of a new man has an independent Christian as well as Marxist origin," Hodges explains:

> The principal Marxist source of the cult of the new man is Marx's "Economic and Philosophic Manuscripts of 1844," which predated his and Engel's scientific socialism. But its immediate inspiration was Che Guevara, who, attracted by Sorel's vision of a morally regenerated proletariat, modeled his own humanism on Marx's prescientific works. In his essay "Socialism and Man in Cuba," Guevara claims that the authentic revolutionary is guided by strong feelings of love, that love for the people is a sacred cause, that to this strong dose of fellow feeling is added an equally strong sense of justice, that there should be ties of friendship only with comrades completely dedicated to the revolution, that there must be no life for him outside the revolution, that there is no sacrifice too great to make for the people, and that sacrifices must be made on a continual and daily basis. (*Intellectual Foundations*, 262)

For Cabezas, the process of becoming an *hombre nuevo* begins with the move from the city to the mountain. The mountain is a symbol of revolutionary ideals for Cabezas, as is evident when he says, "we spoke of the mountain as something mythic, where the power was and the weapons, the best men, indestructibility, the guarantee of the future, the life raft to avoid drowning in the depths of the dictatorship" (*LMEAM*, 28). Discussing the romantic mystique of the mountain, David Nolan says, "many of the middle and upper class students who dominated the Frente's membership felt a sense of guilt over how the plight of the poor contrasted to their own lives as heirs to the bourgeois establishment" (*Ideology of Sandinistas*, 41). He goes on to suggest that many young members of the FSLN took to the mountains to rid themselves of these feelings of guilt. The motivation for Cabezas seems to have been different. He makes very few references to abuses committed by the Somoza regime or to poverty, and he takes pride in saying, "I was from a proletarian family" (*LMEAM*, 10).

Given the mythic qualities attributed to the mountain by Cabezas and others, the move to the mountain is anticipated as a chance to penetrate the mysteries of the FSLN and to work with legendary fighters, but before anything so transcendent can happen, there is an initial shock that makes such goals seem out of reach. Rather than an encounter with the greatness of others, the mountain brings a confrontation with Cabezas's personal weakness. He is exhausted by the sudden physical demands, humiliated by his inabilities, frustrated by the "muddy hell" (*LMEAM*, 61), and tormented by the fear of being detected by government troops. In that condition, Cabezas cheers himself with the following thought: "On my own two feet I was getting closer—I was going to meet those famous men, the guerrillas, the people like Che" (89). The obstacles—mud, weakness, and exhaustion—are overcome by the anticipation of meeting mythic forces and famous men and of becoming like them.

Similarly, the humiliation implied in being called with his companions "useless" (*LMEAM*, 107) and "pansies" (126) is overcome by the belief that debasing experiences remove the old self and lead to the creation of the new man. Echoing many of Guevara's points, Cabezas describes the transformation of the former self into the revolutionary new man in terms of a quasi-religious progression through suffering and sacrifice:

> Among us there was no selfishness. It was as if the mountain and the mud, the mud and the rain too, the solitude, it was as if they washed us clean of a mass of bourgeois stains. . . . that's why we say that the beginning of the new man is in the FSLN. The new man begins his birth bitten by mosquitos, the new man begins his birth stinking. That is the outside part, because inside, due to the violent blows received every day, the new man is born with all the freshness of the

mountain, a man, it seems like a lie, a forthright man, without selfish hang-ups, a man who is no longer petty, a tender man, a man
who sacrifices himself for others, a man who gives everything for
others, a man who suffers for others, and also a man who laughs
when others laugh. (119)

For the most part, Cabezas follows Guevara's ideas closely. He describes,
for example, the new man as a tender man who sacrifices himself for others, while Guevara says that "the true revolutionary is guided by great
feelings of love. It is impossible to imagine an authentic revolutionary
without this quality" (*Hombre nuevo*, 22).

There is, however, an important difference in the scale of the changes
that the two men describe. Che Guevara's concept of the new man is understood as having global validity. He speaks of experiences in Cuba, but
the suggestion is that similar processes can and will occur everywhere as
revolution spreads. He does not limit himself to Cuba, for example, when
he says, "to build communism, we must create the new man and the material base simultaneously" (*Hombre nuevo*, 11). He clarifies the international focus of his project when he says of the "new man," "if his revolutionary zeal is dulled when the most pressing demands have been met
on the local level, and if he forgets about proletarian internationalism, the
revolution that he directs is no longer a driving force and it drifts into a
comfortable lull, which is taken advantage of by the imperialists, our
sworn enemies, who will thereby gain ground" (22). Whereas for Guevara
the new man fails if his revolutionary commitment ends at the borders of
his country, Cabezas envisions the new man in local terms, portraying the
process of becoming a new man as a means of reaching and understanding a specifically national, rather than class, essence. Cabezas takes an international idea and gives it national meaning as part of the effort to naturalize the Sandinista regime, an effort that emerges most powerfully in
Cabezas's claim that "the beginnings of the new man are in the FSLN," a
claim that not only presents the rule of the FSLN as a completely natural
thing but also attributes transformative powers to that group.

With every obstacle that he overcomes and with every skill that he gains,
Cabezas more closely resembles Guevara, but it is ultimately the mythic figure of Sandino who is most important. As noted earlier, the phrase "you
have to be like Che" is repeated literally dozens of times as a kind of
mantra that gives spiritual meaning to the physical struggle, but by becoming more like Che Guevara, Cabezas approaches Sandino, the father
of Nicaragua. In an early passage Cabezas explains the relative importance of Sandino and Guevara through a parodic twist of the Christian

concept of the roles of God the Father and Jesus Christ. Cabezas describes the relationship between the nationalist Sandino and the internationalist Guevara by saying, "yo conozco y llego a Sandino a través del Che, porque me doy cuenta que en Nicaragua para ser como el Che hay que ser sandinista" [I know and approach Sandino through Che, because I realize that in Nicaragua you have to be a Sandinista to be like Che] (*LMEAM*, 23). The ambiguous prose forces two important questions: Is it Sandino or el Che whom the revolutionary should imitate? If, as the first phrase implies, Che Guevara stands between the individual and Sandino as a kind of intermediary figure, why does the second clause reverse this order? The ambiguity leads back to the tension between national and international Marxism. Sandino, a nationalist revolutionary, clearly stands for Nicaragua and the need for a uniquely Nicaraguan revolution. Che Guevara, on the other hand, is the great example of a supranationalist Marxist. An Argentine doctor who played a prominent role in the Cuban revolution and who died attempting to foment revolution in Bolivia, Guevara represents, for both Cabezas in Nicaragua and Vallières in Québec, the global nature of the Marxist message. However, since the task at hand is legitimizing the FSLN as the proper rulers of Nicaragua, it is Sandino rather than Guevara through which Cabezas draws authenticity for the new government.

Cabezas makes this connection through two veterans who had served in Sandino's army during his battles against the United States Marines. These old men, Bonifacio Montoya (Don Bacho) and Leandro Córdoba (Don Leandro), provide a direct link to Sandino, the preeminent figure in the Nicaraguan popular consciousness. The book *Sandino in the Streets* documents through photographs taken on streets throughout Nicaragua the powerful presence of Sandino as an icon and as a symbol of national unity. In an introductory essay to that collection, Nicaraguan poet Ernesto Cardenal describes the hold that the image of Sandino has on the minds of Nicaraguans: "I believe that Augusto César Sandino is the only hero in history who is recognized by his people by his silhouette alone. The silhouette of Sandino is seen everywhere in Nicaragua—on walls, on ramparts, on fences, on curbs, on columns, on bridges, and even on electric and telephone posts" (Prologue, x).

In the two encounters with the veteran Sandinistas, Cabezas and his comrades are mistaken for the Sandinistas of the days of Sandino. As related by Cabezas, the mistakes fuse the two periods of Sandinismo, making it possible for him to claim the confidence of two original Sandinistas and their support of the later movement. In the encounter with Don Bacho, the veteran greets a squad of Sandinistas with the words, "I knew you would come back!" (*LMEAM*, 224). Don Bacho takes the soldiers to a cache of arms that he had kept hidden for the past forty years, long years in which he waited patiently for the return of the Sandinistas. Cabezas underscores the significance of the event, demanding that the reader appreciate the scene. "Do you get it? The old man had hidden the weapons. Do you get it? The old man had hidden the weapons and he took them out every day to dry them in the sun, because he knew that one day the Sandinistas would return" (224). Cabezas uses this incident to emphasize the continuity between Sandino the mythic national hero and the present-day Sandinistas, demonstrating through this scene that the link between Sandino and the Sandinistas of the 1970s is a matter of essence. Although the actors and the weapons have changed, it is as the popular slogan says, "Sandino vive; La lucha continua" [Sandino lives; the struggle continues]. Ernesto Cardenal glosses this slogan as follows: "'SANDINO LIVES'— this was painted on a wall which the Cuban poet Cintio Vitier called to my attention right after the triumph of the Revolution, and which I had not noticed before. It did not say *Viva Sandino*, as the revolutionary and Catholic poet Cintio Vitier pointed out to me, which would have been the more usual phrase, but rather *Sandino Vive*, which gave a more profound meaning, that of an act of faith and a proclamation of resurrection. To be sure, afterwards I have seen this phrase many, many times on the walls of Nicaragua which I noticed for the first time with Cintio Vitier: 'SANDINO LIVES, THE STRUGGLE CONTINUES'" (Prologue, x–xi).

Somewhat later, when the second veteran, Don Leandro, asks about the pistols that the Sandinista guerrillas carry, Cabezas assumes that the old man wants to know why they do not carry rifles, while the old veteran simply does not recognize the modern firearms. Cabezas misinterprets the question, but Don Leandro, like Don Bacho, mistakes these modern soldiers for the Sandinistas of long ago. After his conversation with Don Leandro, Cabezas says, "what a beautiful thing, look, you were touching Sandino, you were touching history . . . and right there I realized what the Sandinista tradition meant, it was reaffirmed for me, and I saw it in flesh and bone, in practice, in reality" (*LMEAM*, 284). Speaking with, listening to, and touching former companions of Sandino is for Cabezas a way of speaking with, listening to, and touching Sandino himself. The intensity of this conviction moves Cabezas beyond his concern for naturalizing the FSLN. Perhaps assuming that task has been accomplished, Cabezas turns to the personal identity that he finds in this contact with Sandino. The powerful sense of self that Cabezas finds through connection with the veterans, and the certainty that through this encounter with them he has in some way encountered the mythic father of the revolution, lead him to the euphoric conclusion of his narrative.

> And then, when I meet that man and he tells me all that stuff I feel like his son, I feel like the child of Sandinismo, I feel that I am a child of history, I understand my own past, I locate myself, I have a father-land, I recognize my historical identity through the things that Don Leandro told me. . . . I had found history through him, I had rediscovered my own history, in tradition, in the essence of Nicaragua, I found my beginnings, my ancestors, I felt that I was its concrete continuation, uninterrupted, I found the source of my nourishment that I didn't know before, I was being nourished by Sandino, but I had not been able to perceive materially my umbilical cord, and that discovery birthed me, I discovered it all in that moment. (288)

If Pierre Vallières finds for himself tasks and roles appropriate for his personality in his revolution, Omar Cabezas finds an entirely new sense of who he is in his revolution. Likewise, while Vallières argues at length against mythic conceptions of national identity, Cabezas draws much of the force of his narrative from the conviction that national myths are valid and powerfully effective on the level of individual—if exclusively male—identity.

Yet for all his apparent sincerity and honest belief in the spiritual transformation that Sandinismo brought to him, Cabezas's depiction of his beliefs is every bit as strategic as Vallières's claim to be completely reconciled with Québec. In both cases, there is a direct appeal to popular sentiment in an effort to link a political program with what is very carefully selected and presented as a national essence. Consciously excluding all those who would advance a different version of the nation, these men imagine their communities in terms that support revolution, not in a general anarchic sense, but the revolution as promoted, defined, and conducted by either the Front de Libération du Québec or by the Frente Sandinista de Liberación National. The vested interests at work in the nationalism of Omar Cabezas and Pierre Vallières demonstrate that the process of imagining the community is not as benign as Benedict Anderson would have it when he says that the community "is *imagined* because the members of even the smallest nation will never know most of their fellow-members, meet them, or even hear of them, yet in the minds of each lives the image of their communion" (*IC*, 6). In other words, we do well not to assume that there is a uniform image of national communion in the minds of those women, opponents, and other compatriots that are spoken for rather than speaking in *La montaña es algo más* and *Nègres blancs d'Amérique*.

4

Nation, Family, and Language in Victor Perera's *Rites* and Maxine Hong Kingston's *Woman Warrior*

The authors of the texts considered in the previous chapters belong to indigenous groups or to families that have been citizens, however discontented, of their respective American states for several generations. Furthermore, with the exception of Rigoberta Menchú and Maria Campbell, the original languages of those texts are the languages that the authors learned in the homes of their parents. The autobiographies in question in this chapter, Victor Perera's *Rites: A Guatemalan Boyhood* (*RAGB*; 1985) and Maxine Hong Kingston's *The Woman Warrior: Memoirs of a Girlhood among Ghosts* (*WW*; 1976), differ from the previous texts in that they are written by the children of immigrants. They are also, like *Me llamo Rigoberta Menchú* and *Halfbreed*, narratives written in the second language of the autobiographer and therefore texts in which language and the need to learn language become central issues. All languages can, of course, be learned, but the fact that official languages like English and Spanish must be learned reminds us that for the immigrant and for the immigrant's child, the imagining of a national community inspires a tense conflict between linguistic, ethnic, and familial loyalties. As Paul John Eakin observes, "while any autobiography, of course, is necessarily based on tacit assumptions about the relation between language and identity, the special circumstances of ethnic autobiography tend to make these assumptions explicit as felt experience" (*Touching the World*, 117–18). Given the vehement complaints of Menchú and Campbell against Guatemala and Canada explored in the first and second chapters, and given the troubled use of nation by Perera and Kingston discussed in this chapter, the "felt experience" of language and the power to exclude through language clearly play a central role in the process of imagining oneself as part of a national community.

This chapter is an examination of the ways that migration complicates the imagination of that national community. Benedict Anderson discusses migration in *Imagined Communities*, but only long enough to reinforce his thesis that national boundaries are permeable. Focusing on broad themes, Anderson provides a fruitful—and unfailingly hopeful—general theory on national identity rather than a case-by-case analysis of its usefulness in understanding a situation or a text. For all the suggestive strength of the concept of the imagined community, migration and the conflicts it produces in the autobiographies discussed here strain the appropriateness of what Gopal Balakrishnan has called Anderson's "almost uniformly positive view of nationalism" ("National Imagination," 63). This optimistic take on migration is most evident in the chapter "Patriotism and Racism," where Anderson describes the "selfless unisonance" created in the singing of national anthems by saying that

> such choruses are joinable in time. If I am a Lett, my daughter may be an Australian. The son of an Italian immigrant to New York will find ancestors in the Pilgrim Fathers. If nationalness has about it an aura of fatality, it is nonetheless a fatality embedded in *history*. Here San Martín's edict baptizing Quechua-speaking Indians as "Peruvians"—a movement that has affinities with religious conversion—is exemplary. For it shows that from the start the nation was conceived in language, not in blood, and that one could be "invited into" the imagined community. Thus today, even the most insular nations accept the principle of *naturalization* (wonderful word!), no matter how difficult in practice they may make it. (*IC*, 145)

By shifting the source of identity from genetics to the historical accident of language, Anderson argues that the fatality of nationalness has everything to do with linguistic identity, but that there is no necessary link between the nation and the biological or "essential" nature of a people. Anderson's argument is a way of insisting that despite our inherited identities, we are not bound to remain Lett, Italian, or Quechua.

Nonetheless, while it is true (and wonderful) that naturalization happens, the move from nation to nation and from language to language is not a simple matter of being invited into a new linguistic community. Simply put, there are complicating factors that Anderson does not acknowledge. To use the terms of Werner Sollors, the new loyalties and affective ties felt by the son of the Italian immigrant for the Pilgrim Fathers—ties based in consent—are a function of a newly acquired language and culture, but those ties come at the price of potentially serious conflict with parents—the source of traditional identities through descent. On the larger scale of nations rather than individuals in conflict, it is Anderson's orientation toward a nationalism of love rather than toward the depressingly familiar xenophobic varieties of nationalism that leads to his overstatement. Although he is a prominent commentator on ethnically and nationally inspired violence, by emphasizing an inclusive nationalism he overlooks the potential for cultural violence, such as the compelled redefinition of Quechua-speaking persons as members of the new Peruvian nation. His eagerness, in other words, to demonstrate the flexibility of national identity leads him to emphasize the possibility of inviting others into an imagined community with little consideration of the price that accepting or being forced to submit to such an "invitation" might carry.

Anderson does much more to acknowledge the difficulties that follow migration in an article published in *Critical Inquiry*. Describing a situation very much like that of the parents of Perera and Kingston, Anderson asks his reader to

> consider the well-known photograph of the lonely Peloponnesian *Gastarbeiter* sitting in his dingy room in, say, Frankfurt. The solitary decoration on his wall is a resplendent Lufthansa travel poster of the Parthenon, which invites him, in German, to take a "sun-drenched holiday" in Greece. He may well never have seen the Parthenon, but framed by Lufthansa the poster confirms for him and for any visitor a Greek identity that perhaps only Frankfurt has encouraged him to assume. At the same time, it reminds him that he is only a couple of air hours from Greece, and that if he saves enough Lufthansa will be glad to assist him to have a fortnight's "sunny holiday" in his *Heimat*. He knows too, most likely, that he will then return to exile in Frankfurt. Or is it that, in the longer run, he will find himself in brief annual exile in the Peloponnese? Or in both places? And what about his children? ("Exodus," 322)

Alone in Germany, the *Gastarbeiter* inhabits a space between communities. Having lost ethnic authenticity or purity by virtue of new language, new experiences, and new resources, he has clearly not gained German identity in the process. Suspended between home and homeland, the migrant adopts a syncretic identity. The travel poster, which combines German text with images of Greece, symbolizes this mixture. However, since syncretic identity, national or otherwise, implies mobility within rather than freedom from history, blood, language, and culture, the migrant and the migrant's child must negotiate some kind of peace between the demands of ethnicity and the possibilities of new national identities.

The case of the lonely *Gastarbeiter* relates directly to the formation of immigrant identity in *Rites* and *The Woman Warrior*. As might be the case for the children of Anderson's *Gastarbeiter*, Perera and Kingston must decide, among other things, to what extent they can imagine their own communities when, for Kingston, commercial images such as Kung Fu movies and, for Perera, hostile religious ideas depict a supposed national essence that would limit them to the identity of mere caricatures. Given the force of stereotyped ethnic images and taking into account the parental pressure to follow tradition, the question becomes who decides what it means to be Greek, German, Guatemalan, or Chinese. Furthermore, these writers must decide if one's home is the place of residence or the place of parental origin. To again invoke Werner Sollors, it is a question of consent versus descent. What, in other words, do the child of the *Gastarbeiter*, the child of Chinese immigrants in California and the child of Jewish immigrants in Guatemala owe to the biological legacy that comes to him or to her by descent, and how free is that child to adopt new forms and modes of selfhood by consenting to identity through them?

The play between freedom and constraint in the formation of national identity parallels the give and take between flexibility and restriction inherent in the autobiographical project. As contemporary literary theory explains, since there can be neither memory nor meaning prior to language, there is nothing but language in autobiography. Language, in other words, is at once the means and the material of autobiography. Furthermore, the conventions of autobiographical writing shape the "I" through patterns and expectations to create a "self" that is comprehensible and meaningful within a culture. As Sidonie Smith states,

> because self-representation is discursively complex and ambiguous,
> a "radical disappropriation" of the actual life by the artifice of literature takes place at the scene of writing. The "I," something apparently familiar, becomes something other, foreign; and the drift of the disappropriation, the shape, that is, that the autobiographer's narrative

and dramatic strategies take, reveals more about the autobiographer's present experience of "self" than about her past, although, of course, it tells us something about that as well. Fundamentally, it reveals the way the autobiographer situates herself and her story in relation to cultural ideologies and figures of selfhood. (*Poetics*, 47)

Smith's argument reverses what we might call the commonsense understanding of autobiography. From a more traditional perspective, the life would seem to be the necessary antecedent of a text that purports to tell the story of a life. In terms of contemporary literary theory, however, the narrative of the life can be said to precede the life in that it is only when the autobiographer tells herself the story of her life that events take shape as a more or less meaningful sequence or progression. Similarly, it is only as we tell the story of our "selves" that the necessarily provisional "I" comes into being. As Thomas G. Couser explains with a metaphor cited earlier, contemporary theory describes a completely new concept of the "self": "We seem to have entered the age of the dot-matrix 'I': that crucial personal pronoun, once impressed on the page by an integral piece of type, is now merely a particular configuration of the otherwise indistinguishable dots that serve to make up all the other characters" (*Altered Egos*, 18). Implicit in the arguments of both Couser and Smith is the idea that the contingency and indeterminacy of the autobiographical subject make new patterns and forms of identity possible. However, as Smith is careful to note, the pressures exerted by culturally based figures of selfhood restrict the range of those possibilities. National identity, part of the complex web of associations and allegiances that compose selfhood, is at once elastic and rigid in similar ways. Therefore, I take exception to Anderson's depiction of the pliant boundaries of national identity only in terms of degree, arguing that although borders can be crossed and although legal naturalization does occur, the children of immigrants, such as Perera and Kingston, find themselves in between communities, in a space that makes a syncretic identity—Perera's father says "heathen," and Kingston's mother says "barbarian"—inevitable. In this "transnational" situation, Perera and Kingston encounter the potential for liberation as well as the restrictions that Michael Kearney describes. "Transnational migrants move into and indeed create transnational spaces," Kearney observes, "that may have the potential to liberate nationals within them who are able to escape in part the totalizing hegemony that a strong state may have within its national borders. But . . . a deterritorialized nation-state may extend its hegemony over its citizens who, as migrants or refugees, reside outside of its national boundaries" ("Local and Global," 553). The difference of the Jewish Perera in Guatemala and the Chinese Kingston in the United States keeps totalizing national identities at bay, but the parents of the authors insist on a deterritorialized national identity that limits the range of the identities available to their children.

In other words, although Anderson, Smith, Couser, and Kearney do not imply that any given form of identity is more legitimate than any other, the parents of Kingston and Perera are not so generous. For Perera's father as for Kingston's mother, national and cultural identities cannot be exchanged without significant loss. For these parents, descent is the central element of identity, and a concern for ethnic continuity dominates their thinking. That their children are removed from traditional Jewish or Chinese culture means that those children are either "heathens" or "barbarians," and that the child is forever different from the parent. The ease with which those children consent to new forms of identity makes life in the new land a culturally dangerous prospect. National identity and concepts such as language, family, and the homeland are serious matters for these parents, and the preference of their children for the place of residence over the place of (parental) origin creates a painful rift between the generations. In a passage that is as true for Perera as for Kingston, Sollors observes: "In America we may *feel* 'filiopietism,' but we pledge 'allegiance' to the country. To say it plainly, American identity is often imagined as volitional consent, as love and marriage, ethnicity as seemingly immutable ancestry and descent" (*Beyond Ethnicity*, 151).

The parents of Kingston and Perera emigrate from China and Palestine respectively with no intention of relocating permanently or of making themselves at home in a new land. The efforts toward acculturation by these immigrants are, for the most part, limited to the acquisition of those skills necessary to succeed in business. This is true since they are in a type of exile in the United States and Guatemala, and since they are more interested in maintaining cultural identity than in becoming "transparent," to again invoke Lugones's term, in their new American situations. The children of these immigrants, on the other hand, move away from the traditions and languages of their parents in an attempt to make themselves less culturally distinct and more transparent. The sign of this rift between parent and child is in both cases the English language. The English that Kingston speaks and the English text of *The Woman Warrior* represent Kingston's acceptance of and by the United States and, implicitly, her conflicts with the Chinese language and traditions of her parents. However, finding the term "American" expansive enough to include her, Kingston eventually contains the contending forces of her American and Chinese identities within that broad rubric. Likewise, the English that Victor Perera speaks and the English text of *Rites* also present conflict between parent and child, but without even the shaky truce between competing allegiances that Kingston achieves. Unable to imagine himself as either Guatemalan or within the Jewish traditions of his parents, Perera turns to the internationalism available through English. Whether signaling assimilation in the United States or failure to assimilate in Guatemala, English stands, therefore, as the sign of both national identity and its absence in *The Woman Warrior* and in *Rites*.

If his English is the sign of Perera's indefinite national identity, his double circumcision represents his parents' failed effort to establish his identity in terms of family and religion. Rather than bringing the child into the Jewish community, the ritually incomplete first circumcision and the emotionally scarring second one create in Perera a sense of distance from the people of which circumcision was to make him a part. It is with this failed ritual that *Rites* begins. "I was not quite six when I was circumcised for the second time because the first job, performed by a Gentile doctor, was pronounced unclean by our new rabbi. My mother tells me that a small flap of foreskin survived the first operation, so that I hung by this integument for six years between Baal and the Shield of David, a part heathen. The ceremonial tableau has lodged in my memory, held there in trust for my understanding to ripen and draw out its full significance" (*RAGB*, 3). That the "full significance" of the botched rite includes a sense of self as suspended between loyalties and identities—part heathen and only part son of David—becomes clear in the portrayal of the second circumcision. Having described the rabbi Isaac Toledano as a man of "Gothic appearance," with a beaked nose from which "wiry hairs radiated like an insect's antennae," Perera says: "His nose is the last thing I remember as he leaned over me, whispering unintelligible blandishments in fifteenth-century Spanish. The rest was howls, astonishing pain, the bitter sinking knowledge that I would never again be whole" (4). The failure of the rite to create wholeness prefigures Perera's later inabilities to imagine himself as a complete member of either the Jewish community or the Guatemalan nation.

By concluding his presentation of the circumcision with the feeling that he is less than whole, Perera indicates that his interruption of a long and distinguished family heritage begins in infancy. Of that heritage he says: "My parents were tradition-bound Spanish Jews, Sephardim. They both descended from a line of respected rabbis" (*RAGB*, 8). That long line ends with Perera's father, who is a merchant in Guatemala rather than a rabbi in Jerusalem but who is still a dedicated Zionist of whom Perera admiringly says:

> In Jerusalem, Father had been a Talmudic scholar and mathematics instructor at a girls' seminary. In Guatemala he began life as an itinerant peddler. (Why Guatemala? Father never explained this to my satisfaction.) Only recently have I come to appreciate the courage this required of him—an educated man of twenty-five, scion of respected rabbis and with only a few phrases of Quixotesque Ladino Spanish, reduced to peddling bolts of colored gingham to Indian laborers in a country so ignorant of his lineage it labeled him Turk and levied on his head double and triple the going rate in bribes, kickbacks, police taxes, and the other routine forms of graft.
>
> And yet he grew to love his work. He took pride in his hard-earned position as one of Guatemala's leading merchants and in his standing within the Jewish community as a loyal Zionist, a scholar, and a humanist. (9)

The problem, in terms of Perera's ability to adopt the traditions of his ancestors, is that in Guatemala his father, although once a scholar, turns to his store rather than to scripture with "Talmudic ardor" (*RAGB*, 9). Consequently, what begins for the father as an expedient dedication to his trade becomes for the son an inevitable absence of training; a bungled circumcision makes him part heathen at age six, but it is his father's overly zealous devotion to his business that results in the lack of language that threatens Perera at age ten.

> Soon after my tenth birthday Rabbi Toledano warned Father that he had neglected my religious education, and said I was in danger of growing up a godless heathen. Alarmed, Father looked up from his ledgers and registers and saw that Rabbi Toledano was right. His firstborn and only son, three short years from Bar Mitzvah, could not read a word of Scripture. This was hardly my fault. Our lingual tender at home was a secular hash of native slang and Ladino Spanish: *"Manga tu okra, ishto; 'scapa ya tus desmodres"* (Eat your okra, animal; enough of your foolishness). Hebrew was for off-color jokes and adult secrets. (72–73)

Much as his Jewishness and the medieval Spanish that he speaks earn for his father the label "Turk," the fact that the young Perera speaks a "secular hash" of languages but no Hebrew marks him, within his family, as a potential heathen. Language, in other words, marks the initial difference of the father from his customers in Guatemala and, later, the difference of the son from the father. Language, it might be said, blocks as much as it invites participation in the nation.

Fortunately, languages can be learned. It is because he is not bound to forever speak an antiquated Spanish that Perera's father can succeed as a businessman in Guatemala. Similarly, it is because he can be trained in Hebrew that Perera himself is only potentially a godless heathen. However, there is an important difference between learning a new language and identifying oneself through that language. Spanish enables Quechua-speaking Indians to participate in Peru (and, we might add, it enables Quiché Maya Indians to work toward participation in Guatemala), but it is surely wrong to assume that competence in a new language erases former loyalties. In the same way, learning locally appropriate Spanish expands the senior Perera's opportunities in business, but it need not imply a loss of his Jewish identity. The fact that languages can be learned provides for the father a means to ensure cultural continuity in a strange new land, while for his son that same principle means that learned Hebrew need not disrupt an identity based in a "secular hash" of languages. Rather than zeal, lessons in Hebrew produce in the son only an ability to mimic sounds. Perera says, "after a half-dozen lessons I succeeded in memorizing the blessing to the Torah, which ends '*Baruch attah Adonai, noten hatorah*' [Blessed art Thou, oh Lord, who giveth the Torah]. On the following Sabbath Rabbi Toledano called me to the altar and I recited the blessing before and after, pretending to read a passage from the scroll, moving my lips to Rabbi Toledano's words like a ventriloquist's dummy" (*RAGB*, 73). Whatever the potential of language to introduce the individual into new and larger communities, Perera demonstrates through his dull mimicry that compelled language learning does nothing of the sort. While an ability to speak Hebrew fluently may never have been the goal for Perera or his father, the fact is that the boy's participation in the rite produces no sense of belonging to a religious, ethnic, or national community.

Despite training in Hebrew, and despite constant exposure to the Spanish of his friends, teachers, and *chinas* [nannies], it is ultimately English that excites Perera's mind and loyalty. His thoroughly unimpressive control of Hebrew is matched by a similarly uninspired study of Spanish, and both are presented in contrast to a fascination with English: "My enthusiasm for English did not carry into other subjects. In all my Spanish classes I was mediocre, or worse" (*RAGB*, 43). That this enthusiasm for English

reflects much more than an academic aptitude is evident in Perera's fascination with American movies and American soldiers, and, most importantly, in his contrast between the Zionism of his parents and his own in-
fatuation with English. "Outwardly," he says, "I was lazy and dyspeptic,
a middling pupil in school, except in English. English was far more than
a second language. It was my Open Sesame to the Promised Land of
Limitless Possibility, just as lavish handouts to the Jewish National Fund
were my parents' passport to *their* Zion" (100). It is tempting to attribute
Perera's fascination with English to a desire to identify himself with a
more modern, exciting, and cosmopolitan world than the one he found in
Guatemala. However, even though we might fault that desire to leave
Guatemala, it would not be fair to expect Perera to fashion an identity
based in the place of his birth.

Making the United States a Zion and a Torah by equating the Jewish
nationalism of his parents with his own interest in English, Perera emphasizes his alienation from family and from religion. Given his spiritual
distance from tradition, neither the Zion nor the language of his parents
is his. Furthermore, Perera shares neither the language nor the homeland
of his Guatemalan peers since, in addition to his ambivalent feelings for
Guatemala, he spends most of his young adult years in the United States
and Europe. The fact that Perera is not able to imagine Guatemala in
terms that include himself gives the account of his banishment by an uncle
an ironic quality: "I gradually lost contact with Uncle Mair, who wrote
me in 1962 to say I had disgraced our religion and the family name by
marrying a Hindu, and I was never again to set foot in Guatemala"
(*RAGB*, 166).

Perera eventually ignores the ban and returns to Guatemala, but he depicts himself as an adult who feels no more at home in the land of his birth
than did the child beginning kindergarten. Remembering his first day of
school, Perera comments: "From my earliest consciousness I had known
I was a foreigner in this strange place, Guatemala. Now, in the kindergarten room of the English-American School, I felt an alien among
aliens" (*RAGB*, 24). Perera emphasizes the lack of camaraderie among
the Guatemalan, French, German, and Jewish children of the school by
relating how the Christian children are taught to view Perera as different. Apparently testing the categories that their parents use and trying to
find their place within them, some of the other kindergarten children challenge the young Perera with such statements as "my mother says you are
a Jew" and "my mother says the Jews killed Christ" (24, 25).

The preoccupation of the schoolchildren with what they perceive as Perera's threatening difference culminates in a violent incident focused on the circumcision that begins the narrative. Surrounded by a gang of boys who rally around accusations like "my mother says all Jews have tails and horns" and "he killed Christ," Perera is unable to protect himself (*RAGB*, 28, 29).

> I kicked and scratched and defended myself, but they were too many. When they had stripped off all my clothes—except my shoes and socks—they stepped back to look at me.
>
> "He lost his tail," Arturo said, almost in relief.
>
> "But he has a bald-headed pigeon," Gunter said. A giggle came out of his face that was unlike any sound I had ever heard from a boy, or anyone else.
>
> I turned toward the wall. My chest ached from the effort to hold back tears. . . .
>
> I cried at the top of my lungs until Miss Hale came. She cleared everyone from the patio and told me to get dressed. (29–30)

By publicly stripping off Perera's clothes, the boys expose what was previously a mysterious difference. In the process, they demonstrate their ability as members of the majority group to make difference a source of shame and rejection. Perera receives the brunt of the abuse in this scene, but a keen awareness of nationality is also evident in that Coco, a French boy, is shouted down and called "Dirty Frenchy" when he tries to help Perera (29). Interestingly, the fact that Perera, Coco, and the other boys address one another in the same language makes it easy to taunt and humiliate, but it does not constitute a shared imagined community of Guatemala. There is more to bridging national differences, it would seem, than the acquisition of language. Alert throughout his narrative to the various ways he is "thick," Perera uses this cruel scene to further his portrayal of himself as not just different within the family and the nation but as prevented by his differences from participation in those groups.

Perera's inability to participate in the nation becomes an inability to contribute to its welfare in another scene. Marching with a group of Boy Scouts to project an image of order in a period of political turmoil, Perera feels for the first time that he belongs to Guatemala. He begins by referring to the French boy, Coco, who did not march. "I pitied [Coco] for missing this experience of patriotism—*real* patriotism. For the first time I felt at one with my country of birth, my homeland, Guatemala. Long live the Revolution!" (*RAGB*, 153). This emotional surge of patriotism rapidly becomes pathetic farce, however, as the young Perera sees that the crowds that have lined up on either side of the street are not cheering him but mocking him.

> We were in the marketplace, and the cheers from the crowds grew so loud I lost count and fell out of step. At the same time an irresistible curiosity overcame me. I turned my head slightly and strained my eyes to the right. Then I strained them to the left. They met with two solid walls of mocking faces and convulsed bodies. I looked again, in disbelief. There was no mistake. The cheers had turned to raucous jeers and hoots. The target of these jeers, and of dozens of pointing arms, was me. When I looked back I had fallen several paces behind the platoon. I realized all at once the spectacle I presented: knee-length trousers, spindly legs, the shortest in the squad by a head; and all of it lagging three yards behind in a now thoroughly demoralized rank of one. (153–54)

The ironic phrase "rank of one" aptly summarizes Perera's lack of community. There is no group in *Rites* in which Perera portrays himself as anything less than out of place, uncomfortable, or actively persecuted. He is the strange and heretical Jew in school, the odd and unorthodox son in his family, and, after attempting to join with his nation in civic service, the one for whom "the illusion of oneness had been shattered" (154).

Perera concludes his narrative with a similarly excluding episode. Having returned to Guatemala from the United States after the birth of a cousin's child, Perera throws a stag party for his former schoolmates. The party is presented as a gesture of reconciliation, but it also provides Perera with an opportunity to portray himself as the equal (if not as the better) of his former tormentors. Whatever his motives, the evening is spoiled by the same Arturo who was the ringleader in the anti-Semitic attack on the young Perera. On this occasion, Arturo, now a prominent surgeon and government administrator, does not direct his anger against Jews but against those whom he considers unpatriotic. He begins with a denunciation of three foreign-trained doctors. "'They are all three unpatriotic,' Arturo began again, sitting down and crossing his thick legs after pouring himself another drink. 'If you're educated and trained abroad, then you should stay abroad. Let the *gringos* profit from their skills, meager as they are. I am a native Guatemalan, a *chapín* of part Indian ancestry, and I take special pride in my mixed blood. I was born here, trained and educated here, and I return the fruit of my education to my compatriots, who need it more than the *gringos*'" (*RAGB*, 191–92).

Arturo goes on to belittle the achievements of his peers, becoming increasingly vile with each invective. He is eventually knocked to the ground by an insulted guest, but even there, bloodied and kneeling in his vomit, he continues to threaten the others. "Because I have Indian blood in my veins you think that makes you better than me? You wait. I'll put you all in your places. I know your secrets, all of you. Not one of you can escape me" (*RAGB*, 193). The narrative ends with the following lines. "I bent down to wipe Arturo's vomit from the carpet. 'And you, too.' The surgeon leveled a finger at me. 'You're an expatriate, and you've paid the price. But if you try to come back, I'll get you too'" (194). The excessive nationalism of the violent and slightly deranged Arturo underscores the way Guatemala denies Perera a national identity. Arturo's is an over-the-top patriotism, a dangerous and authoritarian jingoism preoccupied with authenticity and with the right to claim national identity. Being Guatemalan, a *chapín*, begins for him in birthplace and race, but it is as much a matter of civic duty as it is of biology. The fact that Arturo reserves the right to define patriotic service and to condemn those that do not meet his standard reveals the self-serving nature of his patriotism. Nonetheless, Arturo's emphasis on collective identity through nation highlights Perera's reluctance to portray himself as a member of such a group. Despite the distasteful nature of Arturo's patriotic fervor, the fact that there is no group, nation, family, or language that Perera can defend, even politely, as *his* makes this scene a final statement of his extra-national loneliness rather than a revelation of the vulgarity of patriotism.

Whether to present himself in heroic loneliness or to disparage those who rely on collective ideas for their sense of self, Perera portrays himself from beginning to end of *Rites* as having left the family and as an outcast in the surrounding nation. His outward tendency is met, moreover, by forces that resist his departures from ethnicity and religion. There is some effort on the part of his parents to pull him into orthodoxy and toward heritage, but like the experiences that lead Perera to feel out of place in Guatemala, these efforts, as is most evident in the bungled circumcision, ultimately fail to produce a sense of belonging to family or nation.

Although Maxine Hong Kingston shares with Victor Perera a pattern of movement away from family—away from her Chinese mother, Brave Orchid, in particular—she is not rejected by the nation that surrounds her in California. Because Kingston is a woman, however, her American identity comes at a peculiar price. Whereas Perera never reaches the point of feeling himself to be part of Guatemala, it is eventually possible for Kingston to present herself as Chinese-American: that is to say, as an American who happens to be ethnically Chinese. Early in her narrative, Kingston says, "I could not figure out what was my village" (*WW*, 45), but this confusion as to what group will provide her with an identity is calmed—but never finally resolved—in her embrace of the English language, through her "American" successes, and in the adoption of habits that make her "American-pretty" (12). Her creation of an American identity does not, however, exclude family or tradition, as is clear in the heterogeneous terms that she uses to describe herself.

Kingston's early confusion regarding national identity stems from her mother's determination to override the influence of the place of her children's birth and to make them Chinese by repeating to them Chinese customs, beliefs, and stories. For this mother, the homeland of the child can only be the place of parental origin, and the fact that her American-born children show little interest in China simply means that it must be made more and more present through "talking story," by relating dreamlike, and often illogical, tales of China. Of this attempt Kingston says: "Not when we were afraid, but when we were wide awake and lucid, my mother funneled China into our ears: Kwangtun Province, New Society Village, the river Kwoo, which runs past the village. 'Go the way we came so that you will be able to find our house. Don't forget. Just give your father's name, and any villager can point out our house.' I am to return to China where I have never been" (*WW*, 76). Despite the efforts of their parents, ancestral homelands are for Kingston and Perera, as perhaps for the hypothetical child of Anderson's *Gastarbeiter*, as distant emotionally as they are physically. The parents, on the other hand, seem, in terms of emotion and loyalty, never to have left Palestine or China. Much as Perera's parents feel compelled to return to Jerusalem to die, for example, Kingston's parents do not accept their American residence as their home. Kingston says, "whenever my parents said 'home,' they suspended America" (99). The child, however, whose transplanted memories of China are less compelling than her own experiences, knows no home but America, ultimately making "Chinese" the weak modifier of the more substantive "American" in the Chinese-American compound.

Because Kingston perceives being American as more advantageous than being Chinese, she attempts to eliminate Chinese behaviors and to become transparent by making herself "American-pretty," "American-feminine," and "American-normal" (*WW*, 12, 47, 87). The hyphenated terms express the possibility of piecing together an Americanized self but also an awareness that identity—American, Chinese, or any other variety—is a process rather than something into which one is born or that one can choose and attain once and for all. Mother and daughter work toward different goals, but given Kingston's decision to present herself in ways that are attractive to American boys and Brave Orchid's efforts to funnel China into her children's heads, both women seem to recognize that by controlling cultural and linguistic influence they form national identity. The contest between mother and daughter assumes, in other words, the power to consciously control identity. Furthermore, since Kingston makes herself not just "pretty" but "American-pretty," she demonstrates a recognition that beauty is a cultural value dependent on arbitrary preferences that change with time and place. Nonetheless, despite the cultural subjectivity of beauty, physical attractiveness has very real consequences for the young Kingston. As she says with gently self-deprecating humor, "if I made myself American-pretty so that the five or six Chinese boys in the class fell in love with me, everyone else—the Caucasian, Negro, and Japanese boys—would too" (12). Americanized beauty has potentially dazzling effects, but those unpredictable results must be braved since the alternative is unacceptable. Of this alternative Kingston says, "and all the time I was having to turn myself American-feminine, or no dates" (47).

Beyond making herself attractive to American boys, Kingston attempts to fashion herself in locally appropriate ways by taking two important steps toward becoming Americanized. First, she eliminates those behaviors that violate the standards of "normal" or unhyphenated Americans. These behaviors are for the most part habits that Kingston sees in her mother and that she energetically represses in her own conduct. She says of Brave Orchid's speech, for example: "The immigrants I know have loud voices, unmodulated to American tones even after years away from the village where they called their friendships out across the fields. I have not been able to stop my mother's screams in public libraries or over telephones. Walking erect (knees straight, toes pointed forward, not pigeon-toed, which is Chinese-feminine) and speaking in an inaudible voice, I have tried to turn myself American-feminine" (*WW*, 11). It is ironic that, as Sue Ann Johnston observes, "the apparently more emancipated American culture . . . teaches Chinese-American females to subdue and modulate their voices," even as that culture allows them access to greater freedom and power ("Empowerment," 141).

Kingston's second move toward Americanization is the pursuit of goals and ideals valued by those Americans who do not need to hyphenate themselves. This pursuit, like all of her efforts at Americanization, leads to conflicts with her mother, who views Americans as barbarians and "ghosts." Speaking of the uncomfortable clash between her new American mores and the sexist Chinese attitudes that discount her achievements because she is a woman, Kingston says, "when I visit the family now, I wrap my American successes around me like a private shawl" (*WW*, 52).

Uncomfortable in that Chinese setting, Kingston responds by displaying evidence of her worth in American public life. In sharp contrast to Victor Perera in Guatemala, Maxine Hong Kingston finds in the United States a people who may not exactly embrace difference but who recognize her attempts to assimilate, and whose rewards can be used to counter the scorn of her family.

For Kingston, becoming Americanized is not, in other words, just a matter of being attractive to American boys; it is also a serious effort to find a national identity in which she can be both woman and full citizen. This effort is apparent when, provoked by the disregard of her family for the abilities of women, Kingston angrily asserts her worth and intelligence in terms of American—ghost—values. Kingston clarifies her use of the word "ghost" when she discusses secrets that her parents keep from their children: "They would not tell us children because we had been born among ghosts, were taught by ghosts, and were ourselves ghost-like. They called us a kind of ghost. Ghosts are noisy and full of air; they talk during meals. They talk about anything" (*WW*, 183–84). The ghost is therefore someone—Chinese, Chinese-American, or otherwise—who differs in speech or conduct from the image of the traditional Chinese that Kingston's parents perceive as normal in speech, appearance, and behavior. David Leiwei Li speaks of the wider context for Kingston's use of "ghost":

> The usage of "ghost" for foreigners became a common practice probably in the late nineteenth century when Western imperial powers invaded the Chin Empire of China with guns and opium. For the first time in history the citizens of the "Central Kingdom" were decentered and they strove to retain their centrality by defining their oppressor as the other, the "ghost," the "Kuei" which takes on the meaning of "devil" and "demon." Such negative connotations associated in the English language with Satanic forces are more or less dropped as Kingston opts for the word "ghost" which accentuates the insubstantiality and neutrality of a specter. ("Naming," 508–9)

It is this insubstantiality that seems to be at the heart of what Brave Orchid means when she calls her children "ghosts." The implication is that their foreign experience, the simple fact of living in a new and inferior land, has somehow deprived them of things needed to make one whole.

Countering that line of thought while speaking to her mother—who regards America as "a terrible ghost country, where a human being works her life away" (*WW*, 104)—Kingston argues for the value and substantiality of the things she can do in "ghost country": "Do you know what the Teacher Ghosts say about me? They tell me I'm smart, and I can win scholarships. I can get into colleges. I've already applied. I'm smart. I can do all kinds of things. I know how to get A's, and they say I could be a scientist or a mathematician if I want. I can make a living and take care of myself. So you don't have to find me a keeper who's too dumb to know a bad bargain. I'm so smart, if they say write ten pages, I can write fifteen. I can do ghost things even better than ghosts can" (201). Notwithstanding the statement that her "American life has been such a disappointment" when compared to the mythic possibilities of the imagination (45), A's and scholarships represent an affirmation, through nation, of the possibility of feminine autonomy and of the reality of feminine power and intelligence in that American life. Kingston claims, in effect, that success in an American or "ghost" context negates criticism of her in a Chinese context. The achievement of American straight A's, we might say, counters such Chinese proverbs as "girls are maggots in the rice" (43).

Although contrasts between the American and the Chinese appear frequently, Kingston imagines herself in terms of multiple associations rather than binary oppositions. Through language, Kingston blends the various categories through which she identifies herself to create an autobiographical subject at once embarrassed by her mother's social awkwardness, baffled by her power, and inspired by her toughness; an avenging woman warrior who is alternately a submissive and rebellious daughter; and an alien who is also a participating citizen and the perpetual outsider. As David Leiwei Li observes, Kingston "addresses neither the experience of being Chinese in America nor American in China but rather the experience of being a Chinese-American growing up in the United States. The book demands of the reader, as life demands of its heroine that he/she wade through strands of cultural forces, to understand what is being Chinese, what is being American, and what is being Chinese-American" ("Naming," 498). Kingston is American, in other words, in ways that preserve family and collective identity in the predominantly individualist setting of the United States. As Bobby Fong points out, Kingston reworks traditional myths and creates her own to serve her needs as a woman of Chinese descent in the California of the 1950s and 1960s. She "breaks away from roots only to return. Personal development is not growth toward autonomy, but reattachment to familial and cultural patterns, albeit in new and surprising ways" ("Kingston's Strategy," 117). That reattachment is accomplished through what Linda Hunt has called "the battlefield of language" since it is only by speaking and writing herself into myth that she can approach an identity through family ("I Could Not," 6).

It is her free rewriting of myth and legend so as to construct a self at once independent and obedient, maternal and military, that angers many of Kingston's critics. Apparently convinced that an autobiography must not deviate from the faithful recording of the remembered life, some have castigated Kingston for the incorporation of myth and cultural exotica into her narrative. The "White Tigers" chapter in particular draws the ire of her critics. This chapter retells the myth of Mu Lan with Maxine as the heroine who is trained by a mystical old man and woman and who, as a "woman warrior," avenges the wrongs committed against her family.

It is the imagined, obviously fictional, and strictly personal reshaping of this traditional narrative that has angered some of Kingston's critics. The argument against her reshaping of the myth is that the fiction of *The Woman Warrior* betrays a failure to understand China and Chinese culture, as well as an inappropriate obsession with details that may strike the Western reader as exotic, bizarre, or barbaric. Deborah Woo has argued that those critics who condemn this use of myth and legend demonstrate the fact that "ethnic minority writers are saddled with a burden that mainstream writers rarely confront, the burden of being viewed narrowly as spokespersons for the 'ethnic' experience" ("Kingston," 173). Woo goes on to say of Kingston: "Her artistry per se is not questioned so much as the way she has manipulated cultural myths for literary purposes. Her creativity in this regard is seen to threaten the foundations of Chinese American culture, destroying elements of a tradition which have served as an historical basis of identity" (175). Sau-ling Cynthia Wong makes a similar point when she sardonically observes of the ideological pressure on ethnic autobiographers, "*Bios* is of little worth unless it is 'representative'—averaged out to become sociologically informative as well as edifying" ("Autobiography," 259). By faulting Kingston's failure to conform to a uniform image of the Chinese or Chinese-American experience, her critics suggest that a claim to group identity by one implies a group identity for all. Although Kingston may be too quick to dismiss the claims that others have on who the individual becomes, it is also true that her text has no representative pretensions. When addressing her Chinese-American readers, for example, she emphasizes the peculiarities of experience rather than the generalities of culture, arguing explicitly that her story should not be read as a representative life. Kingston asks: "Chinese-Americans, when you try to understand what things in you are Chinese, how do you separate what is peculiar to childhood, to poverty, insanities, one family, your mother who marked your growing with stories, from what is Chinese? What is Chinese tradition and what is the movies?" (*WW*, 5–6).

The general situation of the child born to immigrant Chinese parents in the United States must have a certain resonance for other children of immigrants, but Kingston is clearly more concerned with those experiences and quirks of personality that make her unusual than in those patterns that make her life representative or connected to a larger family, ethnic, or national context. In addition to the specifying experiences cited above, Kingston identifies with an adulterous aunt whom she calls her "forerunner" (*WW*, 8); she wonders if she might be, as was the aunt, her family's "crazy woman or crazy girl" or "idiot" (189). Furthermore, she speculates on the possibility that her parents' village "had become odd in its isolation" (187), pounding home the message that she and her narrative are to be read as decidedly ex-centric rather than representative. Frederick Buell observes of Kingston: "She explodes the anthropological project by revealing that she is attempting, really, to invent a usable past. . . . Desire, not an attempt to be transparent to an external reality, lies at the root of her constructions of Chinese culture and the past, and Kingston's desires—conflicted, overdetermined, often largely unconscious—are anything but clear" (*National Culture*, 182). Despite Kingston's apparent desire to invent her own story rather than tell the story of all Chinese Americans, the contentious reception of *The Woman Warrior* by some critics demonstrates the volatile nature of the issues that surround national identity. While an autobiographer may create an identity through relationships of consent, others may insist that relationships of descent invalidate that creation.

Those critics who find fault with Kingston's emphasis on the peculiarity of her experience illuminate our understanding of her work by counterbalancing the individual's formation of identity with the weight of social context. Even given her determined difference, Kingston is the product of blended cultures, none of which can be set aside or willed away. The presence of influences that she did not choose makes the persistence of family, language, and national ties as important here as Kingston's effort to redefine those ties. Nonetheless, Kingston's separation or difference and the response that they have provoked highlight the way that their ideological nature makes both group and group-resistant identity subject to question and challenge.

Questioning and challenging at every step, Kingston searches throughout her narrative for ways to establish connections with a past and a country that she must make her own. Interestingly, Kingston's combination of inherited and willed sources of identity is connected to an act of bodily alteration reminiscent of Perera's circumcisions. However, whereas the ritual circumcisions are unsuccessful attempts to mark the young boy's body as part of a group of believers distinct from the world at large, Brave Orchid alters the body of her daughter in an ultimately successful effort to open the world to the child. Of this procedure Kingston says: "She pushed my tongue up and sliced the frenum. Or maybe she snipped it with a pair of nail scissors. I don't remember her doing it, only her telling me about it, but all during childhood I felt sorry for the baby whose mother waited with scissors or knife in hand for it to cry—and then, when its mouth was open like a baby bird's, cut" (*WW*, 163–64). The act of slicing a portion of a child's tongue is gruesome, but the intention is to free the child through an increased ability to speak. Kingston has her mother explain: "I cut it so that you would not be tongue-tied. Your tongue would be able to move in any language. You'll be able to speak languages that are completely different from one another. You'll be able to pronounce anything. Your frenum looked too tight to do those things, so I cut it" (164). Despite Brave Orchid's laudable intentions, the initial results are less than impressive. Rather than immediate fluency, in any language, Kingston suffers a persistent inability to speak. "When I first went to kindergarten and had to speak English for the first time, I became silent" (165). In ways less violent but perhaps as powerful, difference makes the kindergarten year as significant for Kingston as it was for Perera. The shock of recognizing difference (or being recognized as different) is based in religion for Perera but in language for Kingston, who had not needed to speak English prior to entering the public school system. That is to say, beginning school forces Kingston to either assume a new linguistic identity or fail, whereas for Perera, who had already been socialized in a largely Spanish environment, no such change was necessary. Nevertheless, it is eventually Kingston rather than Perera who embraces and is accepted by the land of her birth.

However, that sense of belonging in the United States comes slowly. Since she is thoroughly socialized in a Chinese environment, it is only after years of silence in school that Kingston is able to begin the transition from culturally Chinese child to Chinese-American woman. As Victoria Myers has observed of *The Woman Warrior*, "rather than a virtually autonomous maker of meaning from the chaos of the external world, the autobiographer is plumped down in a world already permeated with meaning (or meanings) and must find what expressions count as" ("Significant Fictivity," 114). Before she can make choices regarding who she will be, in other words, Kingston must learn to understand the languages, structures, and traditions that predetermine what it will mean for her to be Chinese, American-Chinese, Chinese-American, or American.

Kingston insists on a careful use of these terms. In a discussion of the reception of *The Woman Warrior* by "American" critics, she says:

> That we be called by our correct name is as important to Chinese Americans as it is to native Americans, Blacks, and any American minority that needs to define itself on its own terms. We should have been smart like the Americans of Japanese Ancestry, whose name explicitly spells out their American citizenship. Chinese are those people who look like us in Hong Kong, the People's Republic and Taiwan. Apparently many Caucasians in America do not know that a person born in the USA is *automatically American*, no matter how he or she may look. Now we do call ourselves Chinese, and we call ourselves Chinamen, but when we say, "I'm Chinese", it is in the context of differentiating ourselves from Japanese, for example. When we say we are Chinese, it is short for Chinese-American or ethnic Chinese; the American is implicit. ("Cultural Mis-readings," 59–60; emphasis added)

Interestingly, *The Woman Warrior* demonstrates that becoming American is not automatic, whatever the legal status of the newborn may be. The fact that Kingston equates legal citizenship with emotional participation in the nation signals the degree to which she imagines herself as part of an inclusive American community. Her emphasis on automatic American identity and her almost casual reference to Chinese identity, meanwhile, are a clear sign of an ideology that promotes chosen rather than inherited identity and individual rather than group-based portrayals of self.

Of her continuing difficulties speaking, and of the struggle to become Chinese-American rather than Chinese or American-Chinese, Kingston says:

> Normal Chinese women's voices are strong and bossy. We American-Chinese girls had to whisper to make ourselves American-feminine. Apparently we whispered even more softly than the Americans. Once a year the teachers referred my sister and me to speech therapy, but our voices would straighten out, unpredictably normal, for the therapists. Some of us gave up, shook our heads, and said nothing, not one word. Some of us could not even shake our heads. At times shaking my head no is more self-assertion than I can manage. We *invented* an American- feminine speaking personality, except for that one girl who could not speak up even in Chinese school. (*WW*, 172; emphasis added)

It is through that American-feminine speaking personality and through the replacement of her Chinese identity with this new Americanized sense of self that Kingston imagines and portrays herself as part of the imagined community of the United States.

That speaking personality is not a benign medium of expression. Speaking English well and imagining herself as an American girl allow Kingston to persecute the less Americanized. The girl mentioned above who would not speak in school is the unfortunate victim of what Kingston calls the "worst thing I had yet done to another person" (*WW*, 181). Late one afternoon, Kingston finds this girl alone on a playground and assaults her. Beginning her torment with the threat, "I am going to make you talk" (175) and continuing by pulling the girl's hair, pinching her face, and screaming at her, Kingston tries to force speech.

> Sounds did come out of her mouth, sobs, chokes, noises that were almost words. Snot ran out of her nose. She tried to wipe it on her hands, but there was too much of it. She used her sleeve. "You're disgusting," I told her. "Look at you, snot streaming down your nose, and you won't say a word to stop it. You're such a nothing." I moved behind her and pulled the hair growing out of her weak neck. I let go. I stood silent for a long time. Then I screamed, "Talk!" I would scare the words out of her. If she had had little bound feet, the toes twisted under the balls, I would have jumped up and landed on them—crunch! —stomped on them with my iron shoes. She cried hard, sobbing aloud. "Cry, 'Mama,'" I said. "Come on. Cry, 'Mama.' Say, 'Stop it.'" (178)

In her abuse of this girl for what amounts to her inability to assimilate herself through language, Kingston echoes the violence committed against Perera. In that episode, the boys who humiliate Perera expose and mock the visible sign of his cultural and religious difference. Although all the boys involved in the fracas are Guatemalans in the legal sense, the attack is motivated by the desire to reveal the previously unseen difference of the circumcised Jew that makes him somehow not Guatemalan. Similarly, both Kingston and the silent girl that she attacks are ethnic Chinese, but by contrasting herself against the still Chinese girl that she persecutes, Kingston shows that she is no longer Chinese but Chinese-American. In two episodes that support this idea, Kingston demonstrates her ability to defend American ideals against Americans, even though her protests have little effect on the offenders. "I once worked at an art supply house that sold paints to artists. 'Order more of that nigger yellow, willya?' the boss told me. 'Bright, isn't it? Nigger yellow.' 'I don't like that word,' I had to say in my bad, small person's voice that makes no impact. The boss never deigned to answer" (48). Kingston describes a similar confrontation (and result): "I also worked at a land developers association. The building industry was planning a banquet for contractors, real estate dealers, and real estate editors. 'Did you know the restaurant you chose for the banquet is being picketed by CORE and the NAACP?' I squeaked. 'Of course I know.' The boss laughed. 'That's why I chose it.' 'I refuse to type these invitations,' I whispered, voice unreliable. He leaned back in his leather chair, his bossy stomach opulent. He picked up his calendar and slowly circled a date. 'You will be paid up to here,' he said. 'We'll mail you the check'" (48–49). In both cases, Kingston lacks power to back up her brave words, but despite the ease with which her employers can ignore her idealism, Kingston clearly feels that she belongs to America, that she can defend its ideals, and that she can identify those whose behavior places them outside of the "real" America. There is perhaps a greater cultural diversity in the United States that may have facilitated Kingston's ability to speak as an American over Perera's ability to become Guatemalan, but the two autobiographies illustrate the same principle: counter to the hopeful premise of Benedict Anderson, the sign of national identity is not competence in the appropriate language but the power to use that language to define the community by excluding others from it.

Notwithstanding the importance of the power to limit the participation of others in the national community, *The Woman Warrior* is not the story of a progression from a Chinese to an American identity. Much more complex in its development than such a contrast would permit, Kingston's narrative concludes with a tale that illustrates the blended and contradictory nature of the autobiographical self created through *The Woman Warrior*. This tale follows an easing of the tensions between daughter and mother made possible in part by the fact that Kingston "talks story" just like Brave Orchid. The tale is presented, moreover, as the joint creation of the two women. "Here is a story my mother told me, not when I was young, but recently, when I told her I also talk story. The beginning is hers, the ending, mine" (*WW*, 206). The first part of the story describes how Brave Orchid's family survived an attack by bandits because they were in the theater rather than at home. The second part is the story of Ts'ai Yen, a young girl captured by barbarians and carried into savage lands. Kingston links the two stories by suggesting that the songs of Ts'ai Yen, a legendary poet, may have been performed in the theater of the first story. Of this poet, we learn: "During her twelve-year stay with the barbarians, she had two children. Her children did not speak Chinese. She spoke it to them when their father was out of the tent, but they imitated her with sense-less singsong words and laughed" (208). Alone among the savages, Ts'ai Yen eventually learns to appreciate their songs, and their music is the only thing she takes with her when she is ransomed. Her tale, and *The Woman Warrior* as well, conclude with the following passage: "After twelve years among the Southern Hsiung-nu, Ts'ai Yen was ransomed and married to Tung Ssu so that her father would have Han descendants. She brought her songs back from the savage lands, and one of the three that has been passed down to us is 'Eighteen Stanzas for a Barbarian Reed Pipe,' a song that Chinese sing to their own instruments. It translated well" (209).

Ts'ai Yen, whose story parallels Kingston's, sings a barbarian song in Chinese and, in the process, creates surprising beauty through the fusion of cultures. Maxine Hong Kingston accomplishes something very similar by blending (and holding in sustained tension) Chinese culture, American culture, and the English language to create an identity based on a Chinese-American nationality.

When Benedict Anderson asks what will become of the child of the Peloponnesian *Gastarbeiter*, he seems to imply that whatever happens will happen to an isolated individual. *Rites* and *The Woman Warrior* suggest that we must think of this hypothetical child specifically as someone's child and therefore as someone who has—by descent—inherited language and culture. These two texts offer possible answers to Anderson's question, but neither suggests that the immigrant's child will find easy access to national identity. Perera's example reminds us of the reluctance of certain cultural groups to accommodate difference, and Kingston's narrative makes it clear that even a limited sense of national belonging comes at a high price. No matter how eager the child may be to consent to change, the fortunes of that child are inseparable from the legacy of the parents. Shared language makes it possible for an individual to be invited into an imagined community, but language cannot guarantee that an invitation will be extended or that it will come on noncoercive terms. Furthermore, issues of migration and national identity combine to create what Schiller, Basch, and Blanc call "a new paradox," the fact that "the growth and in-tensification of global interconnection of economic processes, people, and ideas is accompanied by a resurgence in the politics of differentiation. When we study migration rather than abstract cultural flows or repre-sentations, we see that transnational processes are located within the life experience of individuals and families, making up the warp and woof of daily activities, concerns, fears, and achievements" ("Immigrant to Transmigrant," 50). Although the increasing mobility of the global population and labor force decreases the relevance of nations and borders in what has become a planetary economy, the strained relations between "immigrants" and "natives," as seen in *Rites* and *The Woman Warrior*, reveal the persistence of national identity on the level of the individual and the family. Similar tensions between cultural "interconnection" and the "politics of differentiation" dominate the autobiographies of Richard Rodriguez, the subject of the next and final chapter.

5

Reading the Nation and Writing the Self in Richard Rodriguez's *Days of Obligation*

As in *Rites* and *The Woman Warrior*, questions of national identity and the individual's relationship to the ethnic group figure prominently in the autobiographies of Richard Rodriguez. Like Perera and Kingston, Rodriguez offers answers to Benedict Anderson's question regarding the hypothetical child of his imagined *Gastarbeiter*. Born in the United States to immigrant parents from Mexico, Rodriguez writes himself through the conflicts between the loyalties of parents to their homeland and the child's allegiance to his homeland, much as might the child of the immigrant worker in Germany if he or she were to compose an autobiography. In Rodriguez's case in particular, conflicts over the reach of group identity and the appropriateness of individual identity highlight the ideological pressures surrounding the imagination of the national community. The conflicts created by those pressures control Rodriguez's two works of autobiography: *Hunger of Memory: The Education of Richard Rodriguez* (1982) and *Days of Obligation: An Argument with My Mexican Father* (DO; 1992).

In their respective narratives, Perera, Kingston, and Rodriguez illustrate the demands that ethnicity, language, and religion make on the children of immigrants. The fragmented identities that these authors describe support the contention of Susantha Goonatilake that "no single subculture has exclusive access to an individual mind, no one culture owns it exclusively" ("Self Wandering," 233). As Victoria Myers says of Maxine Hong Kingston, "the old story does not simply disappear once we have ventured our own design. It remains (and so do others we have made) to compete for our allegiance, as do all the selves we have formulated, along with the selves others have formulated for us" ("Significant Fictivity," 124). The "old story" does not disappear once Kingston "ventures her own design" in *The Woman Warrior*, and the same might be said of Rodriguez in *Hunger of Memory* and *Days of Obligation*.

We do well to remember, moreover, that the task of interpreting and assigning meaning to that old story frequently leads to conflicts between the generations and between innovators and defenders of tradition. Furthermore, both the defense and the revision of tradition are ideologically motivated. Whereas one's ideological orientation may provide more or less compelling economic and moral reasons for supporting one kind of identity over another, personal, ethnic, and national identity will always be human creations, discursive constructs. Given the serious and hotly contested questions at play here, I choose Rodriguez as the subject of this final chapter less for his controversial positions on ethnic identity than for the way those positions and the critical response to them illustrate the ideological nature of authenticity and of communities imagined through choice and restraint, individual and group identity.

Rodriguez's primary concern in *Hunger of Memory* is the construction of a public identity through the acquisition of a language that separates him from his parents, and he emphasizes the pain occasioned by those weakened ties. Throughout *Days of Obligation*, moreover, Rodriguez describes the enduring and competing claims of nation, family, and tradition on his sense of self. Several commentators on *Hunger of Memory* have censured Rodriguez for what they see as his attempt to abandon the culture and language of his parents to create an American public identity, perhaps because he anticipates a primarily Anglo audience. The exchange between Rodriguez and his critics reveals an underlying anxiety regarding the authenticity of those who either disavow or move toward new forms of ethnic identity. K. Anthony Appiah seems to have something like this exchange in mind when he says of categories like ethnicity, nationality, gender, and sexuality, "the large collective identities that call for recognition come with notions of how a proper person of that kind behaves" ("Identity," 159). Condemning Rodriguez for claiming an identity that allegedly disregards both heritage and the potential for collective political action through ethnicity, one critic, Lauro Flores, baldly accuses Rodriguez of being "a spokesperson for the right wing of this country" ("Chicano Autobiography," 85).

In *Days of Obligation*, which Rosaura Sánchez calls "a rebuttal of criticism to his earlier book" ("Calculated Musings," 158), Rodriguez presents a rethinking of the ties between parent and child and an exploration of the ambiguities of Indian, Mexican, and American identities. In Victoria Myers's terms, Rodriguez seems to have accepted that "the old story does not simply disappear," but the mere presence of that old story says nothing about the meaning and use of inherited identities. The sense of self created by Rodriguez in *Days of Obligation* resembles those fashioned by Kingston and Perera in that all three feel to some degree uncomfortable with the languages and traditions of their parents, and all create their identities through the blending of cultures and traditions. Rodriguez, however, is significantly different from Kingston and Perera in that he presents his assimilation into the culture of the United States as the victory, rather than the revision or denial, of tradition. Perera and Kingston do not portray the resolutions of the conflicts that they experience between heritage and change as reflective of a Jewish or Chinese essence; Rodriguez, on the other hand, depicts his American identity as a profoundly Indian achievement. As cynical as this move may be, it runs counter to David Klinghoffer's conclusion that the autobiographies of Richard Rodriguez prove "that the child of immigrants can transcend cultural and racial origins" ("Gestures of Return," 74). Setting up a play between origins and modernity, continuity and flux, Rodriguez discounts in *Days of Obligation* one form of identity or old story by claiming roots in a still older story. Tensions between inherited and willed identities and conflicts over which origins count, what they mean, and who determines that meaning appear throughout *Hunger of Memory*, but they are dominant in *Days of Obligation*.

At times apparently convinced that ancestry makes him who he is, and at others insistent that he alone chooses who he will be, Rodriguez wavers between the poles of independence and belonging throughout his narratives. This ambivalence resembles the multilayered identities that Niraja Gopal Jayal sees as typical of modern society. Jayal suggests that "it is debatable whether the cultural community does or should exhaust the individual," and goes on to say: "The modern predicament surely includes the multiple layering of identities, which may be more or less harmoniously united in a person. Disharmony, discontinuity over time, and a lack of consonance and compatibility between different identities of the same individual are surely possible, even probable. But the plausible antidote to the deracinated individual is equally certainly not the completely encumbered self of communitarianism" ("Ethnic Diversity," 152). Searching for roots and origins to better understand what Jayal might call his "deracinated" condition, Rodriguez asks questions that can be summarized as follows: What is an Indian and in what ways am I an Indian? What is a Mexican and what do I owe Mexico? What is America and how did I become an American?

Rodriguez investigates the meaning and the costs of American identity in *Hunger of Memory*, making claims in the process that have offended many of his Mexican-American critics. Among other controversial statements, Rodriguez argues that education necessarily separates the child from the disadvantaged parent, that a command of the public language provides the only route to public identity, and, in the implicit corollary of these ideas, that ethnic identity delays and ultimately prevents the formation of public identity. Rodriguez overstates his case, failing to account for the fraternity that the ethnic group offers. Henry Staten observes, "Rodriguez's logic turns on a simple equivocation: his equation of the ethnic group with privacy, individuality, separateness—as though it were merely the home writ large rather than another public sphere, less vast and anonymous than the official one Rodriguez has come to inhabit but for that reason perhaps capable of serving as an intermediate circle of sociality between the home and the crowd" ("Ethnic Authenticity," 109–10). We see Rodriguez's rigid separation of family and public spheres and identities in a chapter from *Hunger of Memory* devoted to his years as a student and instructor at Stanford, Berkeley, and Columbia. In this chapter, Rodriguez discusses education in terms of conflicts between perceived duties to family, professional aspirations, and an ultimate unwillingness to think of himself in the ethnic terms that would potentially mediate the public and the private. It is important to note that Rodriguez consciously portrays himself in ways that foreground the social and economic consequences of his individualism. He is explicitly aware, in other words, that by choosing to imitate the life of his *gringo* friends, teachers, and mentors, he is turning his back on those Mexican Americans who will never have access to that kind of choice. Stressing his determined individualism and the loneliness produced by his education, Rodriguez states:

I never worked in the barrio. I gave myself all the reasons people ever give to explain why they do not work among the disadvantaged. I envied those minority students who graduated to work among lower-class Hispanics at barrio clinics or legal aid centers. I envied them their fluent Spanish. (I had taken Spanish in high school with *gringos*.) But it annoyed me to hear students on campus loudly talking in Spanish or thickening their surnames with rich baroque accents because I distrusted the implied assertion that their tongue proved their bond to the past, to the poor. I spoke in English. I was invited to Chicano student meetings and social events sponsored by *La Raza*. But I never went. I kept my distance. I was a scholarship boy who belonged to an earlier time. I had come to the campus singly; they had come in a group. . . . They were proud, claiming that they didn't need to change by becoming students. I had long before accepted the fact that education exacted a great price for its equally great benefits. They denied that price—any loss. (*Hunger of Memory*, 160)

Like those Chinese-American critics who fault Maxine Hong Kingston for the personal rather than ethnic emphasis of her story, several Mexican-American critics take issue with Rodriguez's individualist emphasis in his first narrative, *Hunger of Memory*. For example, two points from lines like those quoted above seem to provoke Ramón Saldívar: the suggestion that Rodriguez can separate himself from his ethnic group, and the assumption that the individual needs a public identity through English. Pointing out how Rodriguez's arguments constitute "a political service to the Right," Saldívar argues that Rodriguez weakens progressive social action by presenting himself as "capable of functioning only as an isolated and private individual, deprived of any *organic* connection with his ethnic group, his social class, and finally even his own family" ("Ideologies of Self," 27; emphasis added). Raymund A. Paredes argues a similar point:

Rodriguez insists that ethnicity is a private, individual matter which is degraded by public, collective exhibitions. As he attacks ethnic activism, he assures his readers that he desires not to abolish ethnicity but only to locate it properly in American culture. His perception of its proper place, however, has the effect of isolating and containing ethnic consciousness, of depleting its capacity for restructuring American life. In treating his own experience of Mexican-American culture, he relegates it to a distant, unthreatening childhood that he may recollect at his leisure and reconstruct as he pleases. ("Autobiography," 284)

Paredes's complaint centers on Rodriguez's use of "ethnicity" in ways that drain its power as a tool for social change. His final point, that Rodriguez treats ethnic experience as something that can be reconstructed as he sees fit, paraphrases the central question in Rodriguez's autobiographical writing: is identity "organic," or is it necessarily an act of creation?

On this point, I disagree with Rosaura Sánchez, who argues, "in Rodríguez's [sic] essays, individualism is seen not as a discursive construct generated during a period of capitalist development but as a transcendental truth, inherent in the very genes of Americans" ("Calculated Musings," 161). As elsewhere, when Rodriguez discusses education, he portrays the process of becoming American as an indoctrination in an American world view, revealing a fundamental interest in ideology that appears throughout *Days of Obligation.* Simply put, "America" and "being American" are all about ideology for Rodriguez. Nonetheless, Rodriguez is chided by his critics in several instances for being uncritical regarding individualism as ideology. While I agree wholeheartedly that Rodriguez is less than sufficiently reflective concerning, for example, the economic consequences of his individualist choices, there is a certain irony in charging him with ideological naïveté when group identity, which is necessarily equally ideological, is presented as the ideal. There is frequent criticism of individualism in the criticism of Rodriguez but, to my best knowledge, no corresponding scrutiny of ethnicity as ideology. The lack is significant. In a similar vein, Henry Staten notes that while Rodriguez does not accurately discuss the conflict between patterns of identity, "neither do those who would define the authenticity of his selfhood strictly in relation to an 'organic human collective' called 'la raza'" ("Ethnic Authenticity" 104).

Rodriguez is valuable here precisely because he challenges the use of ethnic and national identity, ideas that are widely accepted as natural or unchosen. Perhaps the single most important and controversial point in Rodriguez's essays is his reluctance to accept these unchosen and "natural" divisions, categories, and identities. Since ethnicity is a fact of contemporary political and social life, Rodriguez resists that division by insisting on the right not to discard ethnicity but to decide what importance it and other preexisting forms of identity will have for him. It is not, in *Days of Obligation*, an attempt to erase the past, family, or language, but an effort to challenge the often assumed power of these large, unchosen categories to determine who he must be. In other words, Rodriguez's belief in the power to independently determine his identity fades in the years between

Hunger of Memory and *Days of Obligation*, and a respect for the shaping power of ethnicity, as represented in his parents, the Catholic church, and Mexico, tempers his enthusiasm for choice.

Days of Obligation presents a less defiant version of the individual's relation to the group, but a continued emphasis on the ideology of individualism makes criticism of *Hunger of Memory* relevant to a discussion of *Days of Obligation*. Undoubtedly motivated by the belief that the precarious economic and political status of Mexican Americans makes unity and the preservation of tradition essential to any effective effort to improve that situation, Flores, Paredes, and Saldívar critique *Hunger of Memory* from the premise that collective being through ethnicity is at the very least advantageous, if not natural and proper, for Mexican Americans. Consequently, they insist that Rodriguez errs badly by emphasizing individuality and separation, implying that his choices and preferences make him a "coconut": a culturally white man with brown skin. However, by presenting Rodriguez as the "false" Mexican-American intellectual, these critics tacitly offer themselves as his "authentic" counterparts. Furthermore, by ignoring the fact that the intellectual's connection with "the people" depends above all on that intellectual's selective definition of "the people," Paredes, Flores, and Saldívar protect their own status as Chicano intellectuals with the "organic" connection to class and culture that Rodriguez allegedly lacks. Similarly, Rosaura Sánchez and Norma Alarcón refer in their essays to Richard *Rodríguez* rather than to the unaccented *Rodriguez* that appears on the covers of *Hunger of Memory* and *Days of Obligation*. The less than subtle suggestion is that while Rodriguez suffers from "historical naïveté" (Alarcón, "Tropology," 142) in his "self-reflective, self-absorbed musings" (Sánchez, "Calculated Musings," 171), they know both who Rodriguez is and how to spell his name.

When Benedict Anderson suggests that "Communities are to be distinguished, not by their falsity/genuineness, but by the style in which they are imagined" (*IC*, 6), he reminds his readers that we create the meaning of national and ethnic communities as we imagine our place in them. The question of authenticity is therefore moot. Accordingly, I find that the most convincing criticism of Rodriguez faults him for failing to acknowledge the moral and economic issues that accompany his desire for independence rather than damning him for the betrayal of preexisting ethnic identity.

Combining social and economic critique with an appeal to essences, both Ramón Saldívar and Lauro Flores compare *Hunger of Memory* to Ernesto Galarza's autobiography, *Barrio Boy*. The point of the comparison in each case is that whereas Rodriguez has lost touch with his people, Galarza maintains authenticity through an oganic connection with the people. Flores, for example, speaks of the ways that Rodriguez "reaffirms and reinforces . . . *myths* of individuality and social upgrading opportunities" ("Chicano Autobiography," 85; emphasis added), while praising *Barrio Boy* as the life story of "an intellectual who never lost perspective of his roots [or] of his role in society as an ally of the underdog" (88). Like Flores, Saldívar uses "myth" as a key term in his discussion of Galarza and Rodriguez, finding in *Barrio Boy* "an implicit critique of pre-critical ideologies that support the *myth* of innocently separable 'private' and 'public' roles of the self. The interior self that Galarza describes does not exist in empty space but in an *organic* human collective, in what he calls *la raza* (the folk, the people). For this reason, the self Galarza lays bare is not something alienated, exiled from itself. It is his own native folk" ("Ideologies of Self," 32; emphasis added). Whatever the respective virtues and vices of Rodriguez and Galarza, it is noteworthy that Flores and Saldívar insist on Rodriguez's ideological naïveté and on his complicity in the perpetuation of the "myth" of individuality while accepting as natural Galarza's "laying bare" of a self that is nothing less than "his own native folk." That kind of seamless unity, a leveling of difference very much like that seen in Vallières and Cabezas, is necessarily strategic rather than natural, but it passes in the essays of Flores and Saldívar without the first word of scrutiny. We might well ask: If there are "myths" of individuality, are there not corresponding "myths" of communality?

My contention is neither that Rodriguez has found truth in his emphasis on American individualism nor that the critics who emphasize ethnic authenticity see things clearly while Rodriguez stumbles blindly. My intent is not to choose sides but to call attention to the way that these arguments slide toward terms and explanations that assume the natural quality of the forms of identity that they advocate. For example, we might distinguish Rodriguez's sense and use of heritage from that advocated by Flores, Saldívar, and Paredes by reference to the Deleuzian "Taproot" and "Rhizome" metaphors that A. James Arnold develops in his introduction to *Monsters, Tricksters, and Sacred Cows*. Using Arnold's language, I suggest that Rodriguez thinks in terms of "multiple points of rooting" rather than a "unique origin"; in terms of "culture as history" rather than "culture identified with ethnicity"; in terms of "connectedness" rather than a "return to one source" (Introduction to *Monsters*, 5). Rodriguez clearly values this currently fashionable rhizomatic thinking, but neither his preference nor critical fashion takes the image beyond metaphor and ideology.

The interesting issue for me is the portrayal by Rodriguez's critics, and to a lesser extent by Rodriguez himself, of practices and beliefs that are always ideological approaches to and interpretations of the world as if they were natural, proper, and even necessary patterns. In ways that echo what Maxine Hong Kingston teaches her readers about exclusion and national identity, writing about and sometimes by Rodriguez is as occupied with excluding opponents as with affirming a program or an identity. Perhaps this should not be surprising given Terry Eagleton's droll comment: "Ideology, like halitosis, is . . . what the other person has" (*Ideology*, 2).

In a move apparently designed to establish authenticity in new terms, Rodriguez puts a surprising spin on his ethnic identity. He concludes in *Days of Obligation* that by becoming American he is true to his *Indian* heritage. To make this unusual (and suspect) claim, he inverts the traditional image of the Indian as a passive figure "stunned by modernity" (*DO*, 2), presenting in its place the culturally hungry native. This inversion allows Rodriguez to conflate his story and the story of the Indian, as in the following comments made during a 1994 interview:

> It occurred to me that there was something aggressive about the Indian interest in the Other, and that you were at risk in the fact that I was watching you, that I wanted you, that I was interested in your religion, that I was prepared to swallow it and to swallow you in the process.
>
> Maybe what is happening in the Americas right now is that the Indian is very much alive. I represent someone who has swallowed English and now claims it as *my language*, your books as *my books*, your religion as my religion—maybe this is the most subversive element of the colonial adventure. That I may be truest to my Indian identity by wanting to become American is really quite extraordinary. ("New World," 41; emphasis in original)

Rodriguez asks what changes if we think of the Indian not just as the beleaguered victim of the *conquistadores* and of North American and European imperialism but as an active, even aggressive, cultural agent whose choices tend as much toward change as toward cultural continuity. This inversion requires the reader, in other words, to consider the fact of *mestizaje* as evidence of the Indian's desire and choice to survive through miscegenation and through the appropriation of language, religion, and culture. Rodriguez makes an interesting case for this inversion, but he weakens his argument by setting aside the rape and genocide of colonization to argue in ways that present the conquest as a desired and ultimately beneficial confluence of languages and peoples. Much as in his earlier comments on his lack of interest in working in the *barrio*, Rodriguez blithely smooths over the trauma of history to advance his private sense of self and history. Here I strongly agree with Saldívar, who says that Rodriguez "speaks to us from a position from beyond history, as if the dynamic forces of historical change could no longer touch him" ("Ideologies of Self," 28).

Rodriguez's exploration of Indian identity in *Days of Obligation* begins with a passage that emphasizes race and his uncomfortable fit in tradition, in family, and in the nation. Speaking of the heritage evident in his face, he says, "I used to stare at the Indian in the mirror. The wide nostrils, the thick lips. Starring Paul Muni as Benito Juárez. Such a long face—such a long nose—sculpted by indifferent, blunt thumbs, and of such common clay. No one in my family had a face as dark or as Indian as mine. My face could not portray the ambition I brought to it. What could the United States of America say to me?" (*DO*, 1). Rodriguez expands his discussion to include Mexico with an observation and a question: "*Mestizo* in Mexican Spanish means mixed, confused. Clotted with Indian, thinned by Spanish spume. What could Mexico say to me?" (2). Assuming the right and the ability in these passages to speak not just *of* the Indian but also *as* an Indian, Rodriguez connects his late twentieth-century quest for identity to similar searches begun hundreds of years earlier when Europe first stumbled upon the "New World." Read as a defiant challenge, the question "what could the United States of America [or Mexico] say to me?" emphasizes difference, but it can also be read as an expression of interest. What, he seems to say, did Europe offer the Indian confronted with the advance of the cross and the sword into the Americas, and what do contemporary Mexico and the United States offer that Indian's descendant? Rodriguez's face—dark in complexion, Indian in form, ambitious in aspect—symbolizes his view of the aboriginal American. This Indian does not live beyond change or outside history, rather, as a subject willing to become something quite different to stay alive, he participates in and shapes history. Rodriguez emphasizes throughout his narrative his ability to participate in the American nation, but his dark face—race—marks him and keeps him visually distinct from the nation that he has embraced intellectually.

It is important to note that Rodriguez essentializes "Indian" identity, making a profoundly biological argument for who and what he is, even as he argues for the choice to be or not to be Mexican. George Pierre Castile seems to have in mind something similar to Rodriguez's tactics when he laments the ways that the "Indian image and identity have simply been extracted from Indian reality as a 'raw material,' to be smelted and forged into new shapes," referring specifically to the legal structures of the United States that make "certifying the authentic" economically significant ("Commodification," 743). This strategy of claiming Indian authenticity through remote ancestors and through his own self-serving definitions makes Rodriguez complicit in the commodification of the Indian even as he challenges it.

As if unaware of the existence of complications beyond the intricacy of his own metaphors, Rodriguez presses ahead, taking great pleasure in mocking the image of the passive and victimized native, the foil of his active Indian. For example, citing a mournful *New York Times* article on the effects of cleanup money on native Alaskans following the Exxon *Valdez* disaster, he derides the reporter's portrayal of his Indian subjects.

> The reporter from *The New York Times* knows the price modernity will exact from an Indian who wants to plug himself in. Mind you, the reporter is confident of his own role in history, his freedom to lug a word processor to some remote Alaskan village. About the reporter's journey, *The New York Times* is not censorious. But let the Indian drop one bead from custom, or let his son straddle a snowmobile—as he does in the photo accompanying the article —and *The New York Times* cries Boo-hoo- hoo yah-yah-yah.
>
> Thus does the Indian become the mascot of an international ecology movement. The industrial countries of the world romanticize the Indian who no longer exists, ignoring the Indian who does—the Indian who is poised to chop down his rain forest, for example. Or the Indian who reads *The New York Times*. (*DO*, 6)

Contrary to insultingly narrow depictions of the Indian— counter, that is, to the portrayal of an Indian who "seems only to belong to the party of the first part, the first chapter" of American history (10)—Rodriguez presents *himself* as a cosmopolitan and thoroughly historical Indian who reads the *New York Times* and who has dropped more than one bead:

> Let's talk about London. The last time I was in London, I was walking toward an early evening at the Queen's Theatre when I passed that Christopher Wren church near Fortnum & Mason. The church was lit; I decided to stop, to savor the spectacle of what I expected would be a few Pymish men and women rolled into balls of fur at evensong. Imagine my surprise that the congregation was young—dressed in

army fatigues and Laura Ashley. Within the chancel, cross-legged on
a dais, was a South American shaman.

Now, who is the truer Indian in this picture? Me . . . me on my
way to the Queen's Theatre? Or that guy on the altar with a Ph.D.
in death? (10)

With this contrast between the shaman's exoticism and his own fashion
consciousness, Rodriguez compliments his portrayal of the Inuit with two
more versions of the "Indian." The emphasis shifts here from the white
man's refusal to allow the Indian to participate in history to the pursuit by
Rodriguez and the shaman of an authenticity validated by an apprecia-
tive, but very Anglo, audience. In the case of the Inuit and the snow-
mobile, Rodriguez criticizes the reporter and his or her readers for the
presumptuous attempt to dictate what is and what cannot be "Indian" behavior. In his description of himself and the shaman in London, Rodriguez
returns to the question of authentic behavior. Here the scornful "Ph.D.
in death" might suggest that, by evoking an image of the timeless and spiritual Indian for a white audience, the shaman has taken himself out of history and thus out of life. The white audience, meanwhile, can view this
spectacle and walk away assured that the spiritual heart of Indian identity
has survived colonialism and modernization. It is this kind of "Indian"
that the *New York Times* reporter seems to have wanted to find in Alaska.
Playing on the power of those cultural images by juxtaposing himself
against the other two figures, Rodriguez asks if being Indian means only
to be someone whose picture we take or whose performance we admire,
or if Indian identity can also include a well-dressed commentator who self-
consciously portrays his cultural invisibility in cosmopolitan London.

Who *is* the truer Indian? If it is the shaman, does authenticity imply the
staged re-creation of an ancestral past? If it is Rodriguez, what meaning
can authenticity possibly have? If, finally, the question suggests that it is
the urge to identify "true" and "false" that is at issue, are we, the readers of the *New York Times* and of *Days of Obligation*, not being slyly
chided for a preoccupation with a pointless question?

Rodriguez's insinuation is that we cannot answer his question. We can
criticize the staged authenticity of the shaman or the equally staged presentation of the cosmopolitan traveler in London, but these objections do
not bring us to an answer. Rodriguez suggests that his path of assimilation and the shaman's attempt to recapture authenticity through an appeal to the distant past are, inasmuch as they represent attempts to live
in and to respond to history, simply life. If "Catholicism has become an

Indian religion" (*DO*, 20), spending an evening at the theater in London has become an Indian pastime; if "Spanish is now an Indian language" (24), so is English. In a passage that harks back to Rigoberta Menchú's description of herself as woman, Christian, and Indian, Rodriguez says: "I take it as an Indian achievement that I am alive, that I am Catholic, that I speak English, that I am an American. My life began, it did not end, in the sixteenth century" (24). Change is life for Rodriguez. Stasis, on the other hand, whether ethnic or personal, is synonymous with death.

Rodriguez finds stasis in those Chicanos who present themselves as the heirs of the antagonism between indigenous peoples and Spain. Always alert to irony, Rodriguez suggests that this attempt to claim authenticity through cultural stability depends on the very cultural fluidity that it resists. He is unwilling, however, to grant others the fluidity and the ambiguity that mark his own created identity. Of the Chicano movement he says: "*Chicanismo* blended nostalgia with grievance to reinvent the mythic northern kingdom of Atzlán as corresponding to the Southwestern American desert. Just as Mexico would only celebrate her Indian half, Chicanos determined to portray themselves as Indians in America, as indigenous people, thus casting the United States in the role of Spain. Chicanos used the language of colonial Spain to declare to America that they would never give up their culture. And they said, in Spanish, that Spaniards had been the oppressors of their people" (*DO*, 66). Contrary to what he sees as a definition of culture by anchoring it to a place, a period, or a language, Rodriguez claims Indian identity through the legacy of the Indian's willingness to change and to absorb culture. As he portrays it, this is, both on his part and on the part of his Indian ancestors, a true conversion and not what Joane Nagel calls "cultural camouflage" ("Constructing Ethnicity," 163), or a way of masking continuing allegiance to traditional culture.

Basing his claim to an Indian identity as much on the practice of combining cultures as on lineage, Rodriguez concerns himself with those things that motivate cultural change rather than with the faithful replication of cultural practices. This approach reverses Rigoberta Menchú's efforts. Whereas Menchú takes pains to demonstrate her devotion to traditional Quiché values to counter the evidence of separation, Rodriguez defines himself through change. If we were to apply his reading and definition of the Indian to Menchú, we might well conclude that she, despite her anxieties, is the quintessential Indian: an Indian who has chosen life and change over the stasis of frozen culture.

Rodriguez presents himself as having made a similar choice by becoming more American than Mexican. Mexico represents the past for him, and he emphasizes his discomfort with forms of identity based in that stage. We should note that Rodriguez is not suggesting that America exists at some point higher than Mexico on an evolutionary scale. Since he presents the youthful Mexicans of Tijuana as more "American" (optimistic, Protestant) than the Americans of San Diego and the exhausted San Diegans as more "Mexican" (tragic, Catholic) than the citizens of Tijuana, the terms clearly refer to states of mind rather than to nationalities alone. In addition, Rodriguez refers to Mexico City as "the capital of modernity," arguing that

> Mexico City is modern in ways that "multiracial," ethnically "diverse" New York City is not yet. Mexico is centuries more modern than racially "pure," provincial Tokyo. Nothing to do with computers or skyscrapers.
>
> Mexico City is the capital of modernity, for in the sixteenth century, under the tutelage of a curious Indian whore, under the patronage of the Queen of Heaven, Mexico initiated the task of the twenty-first century—the renewal of the old, the known world, through miscegenation. (*DO*, 24)

In other words, Rodriguez is not concerned with either the physical or the spiritual journey from Mexico to the United States or with the socioeconomic conditions in the two countries. Rather, it is a willingness to pursue life through change that interests him. He sees Mexico as the product of such a willingness but also as having frozen change by taking "its national identity only from the Indian, the mother" (12), ignoring or suppressing the evidence of European presence. As an American comfortable with the idea of mixture, change, and impurity, Rodriguez is amused by this Mexican anxiety, but the simple fact that this uneasiness seems strange to him accentuates his distance from his Mexican ancestors. Because of the distance seen here and elsewhere, Rodriguez presents himself in Mexico as an embarrassed and out-of-place American tourist.

His awkwardness in Mexico notwithstanding, Rodriguez depicts a slow progress toward what he calls his father's Mexican outlook. The conflict between the son's American world view and the father's Mexican perspective explains the subtitle: *An Argument with My Mexican Father*. Appearing only momentarily in the form of an exchange between father and son, this argument is for the most part an internal consideration of the extent to which the son belongs to and has been shaped by California and Mexico. In Rodriguez's reading of North and South, Mexico appears in two forms: as the mass of humanity that looks like him but frightens him and as his father. Rodriguez's hesitancy to identify with the people and places of Mexico becomes a recurring motif in the narration of his travels, but on the other hand, a growing appreciation for his father's tragic perspective moderates the narrowly American identity that he presents in *Hunger of Memory.*

Rodriguez begins *Days of Obligation* in Mexico, foregrounding the gulf between himself and his parents' country by basing his first sentence on its effects. "I am on my knees, my mouth over the mouth of the toilet, waiting to heave. It comes up with a bark. All the badly pronounced Spanish words I have forced myself to sound during the day, bits and pieces of Mexico spew from my mouth, warm, half-understood, nostalgic reds and greens dangle from long strands of saliva" (*DO*, xv). By depicting himself vomiting the language, colors, and foods of Mexico, he vividly represents the incompatibility of his American identity with Mexico. Since an assignment from the British Broadcasting Corporation to narrate a documentary takes Rodriguez to Mexico, the point seems to be that it is not a microbe that turns his stomach but the effort involved in affecting familiarity with a land and a language that he has slighted for so long. The preposterous nature of the assignment to find and film a village like the one from which his parents had come becomes apparent when Rodriguez describes himself as "a man who spent so many years with his back turned to Mexico. Now I am to introduce Mexico to a European audience" (xvi).

The absurdity quickly becomes an embarrassing revelation of the broad gap between Rodriguez and Mexico. Rather than allowing him a spiritual return to his roots, driving into the village chosen arbitrarily to represent his parents' home is a graceless intrusion through which Rodriguez measures his distance from the Mexico of his parents. As the film crew enters the crowded plaza, the members of a funeral procession lift a child's coffin from a truck and turn toward the newcomers. Rodriguez describes the scene:

Bobby Brown panted Unh-oh-ahhhhhhhh from our rolled-down windows.

A village idiot—a cripple—hobbled toward us, his face contorted into what was either a grin or a grimace, his finger pressed against his lips.

Silencio. Silencio.

"Turn off the music," the producer shouted.

The production assistant radioed the rest of the convoy: Back up, back up.

There was no room to turn.

The van, the two cars shifted into reverse. Then my stomach began to churn.

My vision of the Mexican village—yellow doors, wet gutters, children with preternaturally large eyes—floated backward. The crowd of mourners in the village square became smaller and smaller and smaller. (*DO*, xviii–xix)

Rodriguez gives his reader a clear signal that there can be no reunion with a past that was never his by using these two painful scenes to introduce the essays that form *Days of Obligation*. In ways reminiscent of Maxine Hong Kingston's complaint that she was expected to return to a China that she had never seen, Rodriguez recapitulates the point of his introduction by saying, "Mexico was memory—not mine" (53). The implication seems to be that although the past influences the present, it can never be recaptured, like a shaman's costume, or returned to, like a Mexican village. Authenticity is metaphorical for Rodriguez, and attempts to make it literal fail dramatically.

Language creates much of the distance between Rodriguez and Mexico, but it is not just an uneasiness with Spanish that makes it impossible for him to bridge time and the absence of memory. Born, raised, and educated in the United States, Rodriguez sees Mexico as a chaotic mass of humanity whose sheer numbers and abundant life threaten to swallow his individuality. That fear of losing himself prevents Rodriguez from experiencing Mexico at anything but a fearful arm's length. When exploring Tijuana, for example, he confesses to a hostess that he spends the day there only to return to sleep in San Diego. The following exchange between Rodriguez and the hostess further illustrates his fear of Mexico, and the ostentatious staging of fear seems as important in this passage as the fear itself.

We stop at a café. She offers me something to drink. A soft drink, perhaps?
No, I say.
¿Cerveza?
But suddenly I fear giving offense. I notice apothecary jars full of improbably colored juices, the colors of calcified paint.
Maybe some *jugo*, please.
Offense to whom? That I fear drinking Mexico?
A waiter appears from stage left with a tall glass of canary yellow.
Ah.
We are all very pleased. It's lovely today. I put the glass to my lips.
But I do not drink. (*DO*, 92-93)

Rodriguez is most explicit when he says, "Because Mexico is brown and I am brown, I fear being lost in Mexico" (96).

The sense of profound difference from those who look like him appears in passages that describe Rodriguez's childhood as well as in those that describe the travels of the adult. In all cases, Rodriguez portrays himself as an American observer who can only look on while others celebrate and simply lead their Mexican or Mexican-American lives in ways free of his self-conscious irony. His crass intrusion into the funeral procession resembles a scene from his youth in that both episodes place Rodriguez outside the Mexican community. Recalling his family's patriotism, he highlights the fact that he does not share those feelings. "At some celebration—we went to so many when I was a boy—a man in the crowd filled his lungs with American air to crow over all, ¡VIVA MEXICO! Everyone cheered. My parents cheered. The band played louder. Why VIVA MEXICO? The country that had betrayed them? The country that had forced them to live elsewhere?" (*DO*, 53). Much as Victor Perera's circumcisions and training in Hebrew fail to establish in him a sense of belonging to a Jewish heritage, emotional distance and time make meaningless for Rodriguez those public rites that sustain the imagined community for expatriate Mexicans. Always uneasy in groups, he opts instead for private acts, such as reading, that permit him to think of himself as an American through the absorption of culture and ideology.

Nonetheless, despite the fear that it inspires, Mexico exerts a powerful influence on Rodriguez. He feels compelled, for example, to try to understand those who shout "VIVA MEXICO!" even if he cannot join the cheer. However, the strongest influence of Mexico in *Days of Obligation* is neither the celebration of community nor the fear of being lost in the Mexican throng. Mexico appears most forcefully as the tragic counterpart of comic California. The subdued wisdom of his Mexican father is that "old men know more than young men; that life will break your heart; that death finally is the vantage point from which a life must be seen" (*DO*, xvi), and the growing acceptance of this belief marks the sharpest difference between *Hunger of Memory* and *Days of Obligation*. This second book reflects the maturity of an older man learning to appreciate limits, as Rodriguez himself maintains: "The youth of my life was defined by Protestant optimism. Now that I am middle-aged, I incline more toward the Mexican point of view, though some part of me continues to resist the cynical conclusions of Mexico" (xvii). The fact that Rodriguez only hesitantly embraces Mexican thinking illustrates the multiple layers that compose his identity. Rodriguez forms identity not by accepting wholesale any one world view but through the slow accretion of influences from disparate and often contradicting sources. We might cynically add that such a process allows him to espouse disparate and contradicting views from book to book and even from essay to essay.

Rodriguez's father stands as the clearest symbol of the tragic thinking that checks the optimism of America. During a trip to Rome with his parents, Rodriguez finds to his chagrin that nothing excites his father so much as a catacomb where he finds a "harvest of skulls." Frustrated by his inability to impress his father with sophistication, Rodriguez says, "nothing I could show my father, no Michelangelo, no Bernini, no cathedral or fountain or square, would so rekindle an enthusiasm in my father's eye as that paltry catacomb he had found on his own. He had seen the final things. He was confirmed in his estimate of nature. He was satisfied" (*DO*, 201–2). The father's engrossing interest in death and finality contrasts starkly with the son's enthusiasm for art, and the episode has the effect of highlighting the son's facile optimism by setting it against the gravity of his father. A second scene places that solemnity in history. Rodriguez says, "when I was fourteen and my father was fifty, we toyed with the argument that had once torn Europe, South from North, Catholic from Protestant, as we polished the blue DeSoto. 'Life is harder than you think, boy.' 'You're thinking of Mexico, Papa.' 'You'll see'" (202).

The contrasts in these passages between youth and maturity, Protestantism and Catholicism, merge with the eventual recognition that life is indeed harder than Rodriguez thought and that individualism does have limits, bringing him to the conclusion that his American identity is a paradoxical combination of Catholic communalism and Protestant individualism. As he says to a group of priests, "we confess a communal faith; we live in an individualistic culture" (*DO*, 197). This paradox sets the contributions of Mexico and the United States to Rodriguez's aggregate self in an uneasy balance in which youthful personal impulse threatens at times to obscure the community, while at other times the rights of the individual fade in comparison to the demands of the group.

The Mexican wisdom of Rodriguez's father supports the Catholic side of this paradox, underscoring the belief in the ultimate futility of individual effort in matters both sacred and profane. For example, in the Irish Catholic church of his youth, a nun teaches Rodriguez that "the prayerful life of the Church is a communal achievement, prayer going on like the tide of the sea. The implication of Catholicism is that man is powerless alone. Catholicism is a religion of mediation. The Church is our mother, because she serves as an intermediary between God, the God of the upraised hand, and men and women, little two-legged mortals. Catholics are children" (*DO*, 181). Rodriguez juxtaposes the austere communalism of

Catholicism with the glib individuality and optimism of evangelical Protestantism, noting disparagingly the superficiality of two young converts: "Two teenagers from Latin America tell me they converted to evangelical Protestantism because American Protestants came to their village dressed in suits and ties. The evangelical appearance advertised an end to failure" (183). His disagreement with the belief in the quick fix, the assumption that the individual determines his or her identity, leads to Rodriguez's skepticism regarding Protestant individualism and contempt for authority. That suspicion is so strong that during riots at Columbia University in 1968, Rodriguez defies the prevailing sentiments of the day to instinctively take the side of the police officers—the symbols of authority.

> Many of the hundreds of riot policemen on campus at Columbia that
> spring ate in the student cafeteria in John Jay Hall. They sat on one
> side of the cafeteria; most of the students sat on the other. I made a
> practice, a theatrical point, of sitting on the blue side, among what
> Catholic intuition taught me to recognize as the side of the angels.
> In the overarching debate I sought the Catholic side. The era's indi-
> vidualism seemed to me to stray too far from the communal need,
> an exploration of limits I privately called by its Catholic name: sin.
> (193)

The paradox is that despite the energy and personal investment that Rodriguez manifests in his defense of the Catholic world view, he is as thoroughly Protestant in his belief in the freedom to form a decidedly unorthodox identity as a gay Irish Catholic Mexican-American opponent of affirmative action and bilingual education as are the converts to evangelism who effortlessly exchange one religious tradition for another.

Rodriguez stages the conflict between freedom and tradition through the presentation of two peculiarly American icons: the schoolmarm and the diner waitress. In his discussion, the schoolmarm takes on the qualities of a kind of secular nun who teaches the common language and culture that make up America instead of the doctrines that are Catholicism. Rodriguez's portrayal of this teacher as "a minor villain" (*DO*, 172) stresses the ambivalence of individualist America for the common culture that she teaches.

> In the nineteenth century, even as the American city was building,
> Samuel Clemens romanced the nation with a celebration of the wild-
> ness of the American river, the eternal rejection of school and shoes.

> But in the red brick cities, and on streets without trees, the river be-
> came an idea, a learned idea, a shared idea, a civilizing idea, talking
> all to itself. Women, usually women, stood in front of rooms crowded
> with the children of immigrants, teaching those children a common
> language. For language is not just another classroom skill, as today's
> bilingualists would have it. Language is *the* lesson of grammar school.
> And from the schoolmarm's achievement came the possibility of a
> shared history and a shared future. To my mind, this achievement was
> an honorable one, comparable to the opening of the plains, the build-
> ing of bridges. Grammar-school teachers forged a nation. (163)

Rodriguez's argument is that we can speak of the archetypal American quality of Huck Finn's shoeless rebellion because the schoolmarm has taught us to value the river. In other words, America's common culture does not spring from the land it occupies or from some essential trait of its citizens but from the way Americans have been taught in school to view and act on that land. According to Werner Sollors, "America" comes into being as we, generation after generation, consent to "American" ideology. It is ideology and consent rather than biology and descent that make it possible for us to speak of an American nation. Furthermore, it is ideology and consent rather than, in Rosaura Sánchez's terms, "a transcendental truth, inherent in the very genes of Americans" ("Calculated Musings," 161), that make it possible for us to speak of an American Richard Rodriguez.

However, ideology and language must be learned, and the fact that schools across the continent teach them implicates students of all racial, ethnic, and language backgrounds in the imagining that creates America anew for each generation. It is with Americans as it was with Europeans after the advent of print languages. According to Benedict Anderson, those Europeans "gradually became aware of the hundreds of thousands, even millions, of people in their particular language-field, and at the same time that *only those* hundreds of thousands, or millions, so belonged. These fellow-readers, to whom they were connected through print, formed, in their secular, particular, visible invisibility, the embryo of the nationally imagined community" (*IC*, 44). Instructing their pupils in the language and ideas that define America, schoolteachers forge the nation. Moreover, just as the teachers of earlier centuries played a central role in the initial imagining of the nation, the work of their heirs in the twentieth century made it inevitable that *Ricardo Rodríguez* would join in that process and thus become *Richard Rodriguez*. For the child of immigrants in the United

States, becoming American has nothing to do with choice because America's ideology is inescapable, and Rodriguez insists that all attempts to hold America at bay through ethnic, family, or linguistic identity will fail.

> The child of immigrant parents is supposed to perch on a hyphen, taking only the dose of America he needs to advance in America.
>   At the family picnic, the child wanders away from the spiced food and faceless stories to watch some boys playing baseball in the distance. (*DO*, 159)

>   Immigrant parents send their children to school (simply, they think) to acquire the skills to "survive" in America. But the child returns home as America. Foolish immigrant parents. (173)

Speaking of the immigrant Peloponnesian in Germany, Benedict Anderson asks, "and what about his children?" ("Exodus," 322). Rodriguez answers quite simplistically, stating flatly that the child of immigrants from Mexico living in the United States inevitably becomes an American. The pervasive quality of American popular culture motivates Rodriguez's conviction to some degree, but he grounds his conviction primarily in education: an education that teaches the child that he or she belongs to a culture defined by rebellion against authority, by slavery, by the tragedy of cowboys and Indians, and by Puritan emphasis on the individual will. Since learning the value of independent thought and of rebellion against authority is central in this process, those who attempt to reject American identity merely confirm the strength of its ideology. Rodriguez says, "no belief is more cherished by Americans, no belief is more typical of America, than the belief that one can choose to be free of American culture" (*DO*, 171).

However, that one can defy history to make a new start independent of whatever inspires rebellion, disappointment, or offense is the message of Rodriguez's second distinctly American icon: the diner waitress. Directly opposed to his concept of the schoolmarm but created by her lesson that there is a common culture that defines even the most rebellious American, the waitress exalts the freedom of the individual with the wipe of a rag.

> She is the priestess of the short order, curator of the apple pie. She administers all the consolation of America. She has no illusions. She knows the score; she hands you the Bill of Rights printed on plastic, decorated with a heraldic tumble of French fries and drumsticks and steam.

Your table may yet be littered with bitten toast and spilled coffee and a dollar tip. Now you will see the greatness of America. As one complete gesture, the waitress pockets the tip, stacks dishes along one strong forearm, produces a damp rag soaked in lethe water, which she then passes over the Formica.

There! With that one swipe of the rag, the past has been obliterated. The Formica gleams like new. You can order anything you want. (*DO*, 54–55)

Beneath the damp Formica veneer and disguised by the youth painted on the waitress's cheeks lies the deception of this vision of America. The strong arm of the waitress removes the evidence of prior customers, promoting the illusion that a new diner may order and eat his or her meal free of both the past and the future. Since the customer neither clears away the picked-over remnants of earlier meals nor cleans the soiled plates and table of his or her own meal, each patron can consider him- or herself a discrete individual rather than one of the hundreds that have warmed the vinyl seat, smeared gravy on the table, and ground French fries into the stained carpet.

Similarly, it is because America promotes the illusion of an obliterated past that the child of immigrants can aspire to anything he or she wants. When Rodriguez says to his reader, "you will find yourself a stranger to your parents, a stranger to your own memory of yourself" (*DO*, 161), it is perhaps because he realizes that the Americanized "I" who wrote *Hunger of Memory* attempted to wipe the Mexican "I" of childhood from the table of identity. Americanization is a thorough process, and even the best efforts of the more mature "I" of *Days of Obligation* will not be enough to recover what was lost. Nonetheless, the past endures our best efforts to erase it, making an Americanized autobiographical self more of a palimpsest than a clean table. Even if "America is the country where one stops being Italian or Chinese or German" (164), the memory of a different identity and understanding of the world lingers. Given this, we might alter Benedict Anderson's take on immigrants and their children. Whereas he maintains that "if I am a Lett, my daughter may be an Australian. The son of an Italian immigrant to New York will find ancestors in the Pilgrim Fathers" (*IC*, 145), Kingston, Perera, and Rodriguez suggest that the assimilation cannot be complete. Speaking, for example, of the knowledge that he has not always been American, Rodriguez remembers change. "When I was a boy who spoke Spanish, I saw America whole. I realized that there was a culture here because I lived apart from it. I didn't like

America. Then I entered the culture. I entered the culture as you did, by going to school. I became Americanized. I ended up believing in choices as much as any of you do" (*DO*, 172). For all the compelling quality of choice and freedom as ideals, there is no such thing as the freedom to choose ancestry. Likewise, no one has the power to determine how others view the decision to assimilate. An identity perceived subjectively by the assimilated as a victory may, therefore, be seen by others as a pathetic sham. It is this ideologically charged interplay between the individual, the nation, and the ethnic group that makes these questions of identity more complicated than they often appear in Rodriguez's narratives. In *Days of Obligation*, the persistence of ethnic identity becomes an accusation when Mexico considers the *pocho*, the assimilated—and unauthentic—(Mexican) American. Completing his metaphor of the diner table, Rodriguez says, "when we return to Mexico as *turistas*, with our little wads of greenbacks, our credit cards, our Japanese cameras, our Bermuda shorts, our pauses for directions and our pointing fingers, Mexico condescends to take our order (our order in halting Spanish), *claro señor*. But the table is not cleared; the table will never be cleared. Mexico prefers to reply in English, as a way of saying: *¡Pocho!*" (58).

America promises a new beginning, freedom from the past, and a clean table; Mexico defers to the new American with biting sarcasm—the table will never be cleared. The impasse remains unresolved, but the melancholy realization that his father correctly believes that "much in life is failure or compromise" links these divergent views for Rodriguez (*DO*, 219). In other words, even if it is inevitable that the American child will believe in choice, it is by no means inevitable that the child will succeed. Apparently believing more in what Niraja Gopal Jayal calls the "multiple layering of identities" than in the power to write himself independently of them, Rodriguez creates in *Days of Obligation* a complex Mexican, Indian, and American self for whom anything but disharmony and a lack of continuity over time would be the best evidence of a truly deracinated condition.

Conclusion: The Tools of the
National Imagination

Although basic building blocks of national identity such as language, territory, shared history, and ethnicity change relatively little from text to text, my focus on the act of imagining the national community highlights the impressively varied responses to that fairly constant impulse. I am struck, in other words, not only by the ubiquity of national identity but also by the diversity of the forms that it takes. Stable in its general outlines, the sense of belonging in a nation varies widely both in the forms that it takes and in its uses. As Ulf Hannerz observes,

> As far as the nation is concerned, it is undoubtedly true . . . that
> it seems often to be constructed with the same tool kit of ideas and
> symbols, recurring in different places. Yet the tools of identity and
> imagination may not always be equally available to all nation builders,
> nor are the contexts of assembling, disassembling or reconstructing
> all the same. At the very same time as globalization may lead us to
> rethink the notion of the nation in one array of instances, and perhaps
> look for signs of organizational or symbolic decay, in other cases
> nations and nationalism appear to be on an upswing. ("Withering
> Away," 389)

Indeed, for every situation in which the individual is able to construct him- or herself in terms beyond the borders of ethnicity, there seem to be several situations that compel the opposite reaction: a return to ethnic and national differentiation.

Anthony Smith claims that this return to nation is not necessarily the xenophobic evil of "ethnic-cleansing" but is in fact "the only realistic basis for a free society of states in the modern world" ("Culture," 147). Smith insists that "it would be folly to predict an early supersession of nationalism and an imminent transcendence of the nation," because "both remain indispensable elements of an interdependent world and mass-communications culture. For a global culture seems unable to offer the qualities of collective faith, dignity and hope that only a 'religion surrogate,' with its promise of a territorial culture-community across the generations, can provide" (*Nations and Nationalism*, 160). Similarly, Benedict Anderson asks his readers to remember that "nations inspire love, and often profoundly self-sacrificing love" (*IC*, 141).

Perhaps the best summary of my use of the work of Anderson, Smith, and others is that we, like the nine autobiographers read and compared in the previous five chapters, are all necessarily the "nation builders" that Hannerz describes. The fact that potential compatriots create the nation as they come to believe that they are a community means that there will always be a broad diversity of national forms from nation to nation, but also that there can be no guarantee of uniform imagination within the nation. Because access to the "tools of identity" varies from generation to generation, from region to region, and, importantly, from gender to gender, children imagine their national, ethnic, or religious community differently than do their parents; indigenous groups emphasize their marginality relative to the dominant nation; and minority groups challenge the right of the state to represent the nation. In short, the nine autobiographical narratives considered here illustrate both the liberating potential of seeing the nation as the product of its citizens and the instability that follows the creation and stretching of the boundaries of the imagined community.

Notes

1 Rigoberta Menchú and Survival Culture in Guatemala

1. The mediating role of the editor-ethnologist is one of the great mysteries of Menchú's "as-told-to" narrative. Elizabeth Burgos, the editor and organizer of the text, shaped the narrative in important ways but has left no record of the questions she asked, the material she has omitted, or the extent to which she has changed the language and ideas of Rigoberta Menchú to make them more palatable to her audience. For a review of mediation in *Me llamo Rigoberta Menchú*, see Elzbieta Sklodowska, "Testimonio mediatizado."

Menchú's narrative is commonly read and discussed as a *testimonio*, an example of testimonial literature. For an introduction to the genre, see John Beverley ("Margin at the Center" and "Through All Things Modern"). The most important collection of criticism on *testimonio* is Georg Gugelberger's *The Real Thing: Testimonial Discourse and Latin America*. See in particular the contributions of George Yúdice ("*Testimonio* and Postmodernism"), Santiago Colás ("What's Wrong") and John Beverley ("The Real Thing").

For discussion of the heterogeneous nature of testimonial narrative and of differences between autobiography and *testimonio*, see Rosemary Geisdorfer-Feal ("Spanish American Ethnobiography"), Hugo Achugar ("Notas sobre"), and Doris Sommer ("Not Just a Personal Story").

2 State, National, and Gender Identity

1. Sylvia Bowerbank and Dolores Nawagesi Wawia explain that there are four categories for persons of native ancestry in Canada: "(1) status Indians (those with inherent rights within the 1876 Indian Act); (2) nonstatus Indians; (3) the Métis, who are of mixed parentage (Indian and non-Indian); and (4) the Inuit (or Eskimo)" ("Literature and Criticism," 581). It is a combination of the government's creations of these categories and Campbell's discomfort in the only category that is appropriate to her (Métis) that produces the conflicts regarding personal identity in *Halfbreed*. Campbell uses three terms to refer to her people: Halfbreed, Métis, and Road Allowance people. I follow her practice in using the terms interchangeably.

2. Nyrop and Weil's *Brazil: A Country Study* gives the following information on the *favelas*: "*Favelas* have been damned by conservative and reformer alike as cesspools of corruption, decay, and social disintegration. There can be no doubt that the standard of living in the *favelas* is marginal. Access to water and electricity is frequently limited. In the worst *favelas* unsanitary conditions, overcrowding, and poor nutrition have led to rampant disease and high rates of infant mortality. Those in industrial areas are subject to levels of pollution that almost defy description" (*Brazil*, 137). The authors go on to say, "many *favelas* have a high level of social cohesion and an effective system of mutual assistance. *Favelados* can rely on their neighbors for small loans, babysitting, the use of space in their refrigerators, help in making small improvements on their houses, and the like. Nearly three-quarters of *favelados* surveyed in the early 1970s belonged to one or more *favela* associations. Far from representing the nadir of social disorganization, most *favelas* show a careful husbanding of extremely limited resources" (137).

3. De Jesus's metaphors for the *favela* include the following:

> "Estou no quarto de despejo, e o que está no quarto de despejo ou quema-se ou joga-se no lixo" (*QD*, 37) [I'm in the trash bin, and whatever is in the trash bin is either burned or thrown out].

> "Isto aqui é lugar para os porcos. Mas se puzessem os porcos aqui, haviam de protestar e fazer greve" (*QD*, 51) [This is a place for pigs. But if they were to put pigs in here, they would protest and go on strike].

> "A favela é uma cidade esquisita e o prefeito daqui é o Diabo" (*QD*, 99) [The *favela* is a strange city and the mayor of it is the Devil].

"Favela, sucursal do Inferno, ou o propio Inferno" (*QD*, 184)
[*Favela*, branch of Hell, if not Hell itself] (*Child of the Dark*, 140).

"É por isso que eu digo que a favela é o chiqueiro de São Paulo"
(*QD*, 199) [That's why I say that the *favela* is the dungheap of
São Paulo].

4. Herbert S. Klein writes that the International Monetary Fund (IMF)
"Stabilization Plan" for the Bolivian economy "required that Bolivia balance
its budget, end the food subsidization of the miners, hold down wage increases, create a single exchange rate, and adopt a host of other measures restricting government initiatives and expenditures. Even by the usual IMF standards, the Bolivian plan was an extreme one, envisioning the creation of a
stable currency with almost zero inflationary growth within the space of one
or two years" (*Bolivia*, 242).

3 Myths of Revolution and National in Pierre Vallières and Omar Cabezas

1. Regarding Vallières's continuing interest in religion, Malcolm Reid describes Vallières's activities over the past several years, noting that he (Vallières)
has "turned his attention to . . . Ecology. The theology of liberation. A certain
glimpse of non-violence. Base communities. Affinity groups. The Amerindian
movement." In addition, "he helped edit a longstanding publication of the
Catholic Left, *Vie Ouvrière*. . . . For Pierre Vallières had discovered his religion" ("Adventures," 18).

Bibliography

Achugar, Hugo. "Notas sobre el discurso testimonial latinoamericano." In *La historia en la literatura iberoamericana*, ed. Raquel Chang-Rodríguez and Gabriella de Beer, 280–94. New York: Ediciones del Norte, 1989.

Alarcón, Norma. "Tropology of Hunger: The 'Miseducation' of Richard Rodríguez." In *The Ethnic Canon: Histories, Institutions, and Interventions*, ed. David Palumbo-Liu, 140–52. Minneapolis: Univ. of Minnesota Press, 1995.

Amar Sánchez, Ana María. "La ficción del testimonio." *Revista Iberoamericana* 56, no. 151 (April–June 1990): 447–61.

Anderson, Benedict. "Exodus." *Critical Inquiry* 20 (winter 1994): 314–27.

———. *Imagined Communities: Reflections on the Origin and Spread of Nationalism*. Rev. ed. New York: Verso, 1994.

"Announcement of Peace Prize." *New York Times*, 17 Oct. 1992, A5.

Appiah, Anthony K. "Identity, Authenticity, Survival: Multicultural Societies and Social Reproduction." In *Multiculturalism: Examining the Politics of Recognition*, ed. Amy Gutmann, 149–63. Princeton: Princeton Univ. Press, 1994.

Arbós, Xavier. "'Nation-State': The Range and Future of a Concept." *Canadian Review of Studies in Nationalism* 17, nos. 1–2 (1990): 61–68.

Arnold, A. James. Introduction to *Monsters, Tricksters, and Sacred Cows: Animal Tales and American Identities*, ed. A. James Arnold, 1–22. Charlottesville: Univ. Press of Virginia, 1996.

Balakrishnan, Gopal. "The National Imagination." *New Left Review* 211 (May–June 1995): 56–68.

Bataille, Gretchen M., and Kathleen Mullen Sands. *American Indian Women: Telling Their Lives*. Lincoln: Univ. of Nebraska Press, 1984.

Beevor, Anthony. "The Last Marine and the Guerrilleros." *Books and Bookmen* 359 (Sept. 1985): 13–14.

Beverley, John. "The Margin at the Center: On *Testimonio* (Testimonial Narrative)." *Modern Fiction Studies* 35, no. 1 (1989): 11–28.

——. "The Real Thing." In *The Real Thing: Testimonial Discourse and Latin America*, ed. Georg Gugelberger, 266–86. Durham: Duke Univ. Press, 1996.

——. "'Through All Things Modern': Second Thoughts on *Testimonio*." *boundary 2* 18, no. 2 (summer 1991): 1–21.

Beverley, John, and Marc Zimmerman. *Literature and Politics in the Central American Revolutions*. Austin: Univ. of Texas Press, 1990.

Bowerbank, Sylvia, and Dolores Nawagesi Wawia. "Literature and Criticism by Native and Métis Women in Canada." *Feminist Studies* 20 (1994): 565–81.

Buell, Frederick. *National Culture and the New Global System*. Baltimore: Johns Hopkins Univ. Press, 1994.

Burgos, Elizabeth, ed. *Me llamo Rigoberta Menchú y así me nació la conciencia*. 1983. Reprint, Mexico City: Siglo Veintiuno Editores, 1991.

Buss, Helen M. *Mapping Ourselves: Canadian Women's Autobiography in English*. Montreal: McGill-Queen's Univ. Press, 1993.

Cabezas, Omar. *La montaña es algo más que una inmensa estepa verde*. 1982. Reprint, Mexico City: Siglo Veintiuno Editores, 1990.

Campbell, Maria. *Halfbreed*. Toronto: McClelland & Stewart, 1973.

Cardenal, Ernesto. Prologue to *Sandino in the Streets*, ed. Joel C. Sheesley and Wayne G. Bragg, x–xii. Bloomington: Indiana Univ. Press, 1991.

Castile, George Pierre. "The Commodification of Indian Identity." *American Anthropologist* 98, no. 4 (Dec. 1996): 743–49.

Christian, Shirley. *Nicaragua: Revolution in the Family*. New York: Random House, 1985.

Chungara, Domitila. "The Owners of This Land . . . : An Interview with Domitila Chungara." Interview by Aníbal Yáñez. *Latin American Perspectives* 19, no. 3 (summer 1992): 92–103.

Colás, Santiago. "What's Wrong with Representation? *Testimonio* and Democratic Culture." In *The Real Thing: Testimonial Discourse and Latin America*, ed. Georg Gugelberger, 161–71. Durham: Duke Univ. Press, 1996.

Connor, Walker. "The Nation and Its Myth." *International Journal of Comparative Sociology* 33, nos. 1–2 (1992): 48–57.

Couser, G. Thomas. *Altered Egos: Authority in American Autobiography.* New York: Oxford Univ. Press, 1989.

Davis, Lisa. "An Invitation to Understanding among Poor Women of the Americas: *The Color Purple* and *Hasta no verte Jesús mío.*" In *Reinventing the Americas: Comparative Studies of Literature of the United States and Spanish America*, ed. Bell Gale Chevigny and Gari Laguardia, 224–41. New York: Cambridge Univ. Press, 1986.

de Man, Paul. "Autobiography as De-facement." *MLN* 94 (1979): 919–30.

Dickinson, John A., and Brian Young. *A Short History of Quebec.* Toronto: Copp Clark Pitman, 1993.

Eagleton, Terry. *Ideology: An Introduction.* London: Verso, 1991.

Eakin, Paul John. *Touching the World: Reference in Autobiography.* Princeton: Princeton Univ. Press, 1992.

Flores, Lauro. "Chicano Autobiography: Culture, Ideology and the Self." *Americas Review* 18, no. 2 (1990): 80–91.

Fong, Bobby. "Maxine Hong Kingston's Autobiographical Strategy in *The Woman Warrior.*" *Biography* 12, no. 2 (spring 1989): 116–26.

Gagnon, Alain, and Mary Montcalm. *Quebec: Beyond the Quiet Revolution.* Scarborough ON: Nelson Canada, 1990.

Geisdorfer-Feal, Rosemary. "Spanish American Ethnobiography and the Slave Narrative Tradition: *Biografía de un cimarrón* and *Me llamo Rigoberta Menchú.*" *Modern Language Studies* 20, no. 1 (winter 1990): 100–111.

Goonatilake, Susantha. "The Self Wandering between Cultural Localization and Globalization." In *The Decolonization of Imagination: Culture, Knowledge, and Power*, ed. Jan Nederveen Pieterse and Bhikhu Parekh, 225–39. London: Zed Books, 1995.

Guevara, Ernesto. *El hombre nuevo.* Mexico City: Universidad Nacional Autónoma de México, 1978.

Gugelberger, Georg. "Institutionalization of Transgression: Testimonial Discourse and Beyond." In *The Real Thing: Testimonial Discourse and Latin America*, ed. Georg Gugelberger, 1–19. Durham: Duke Univ. Press, 1996.

Guindon, Hubert. *Quebec Society: Tradition, Modernity, and Nationhood.* Toronto: Univ. of Toronto Press, 1988.

Hannerz, Ulf. "The Withering Away of the Nation?" *Ethnos* 58, nos. 3–4 (1993): 377–91.

Hobsbawm, Eric. "Inventing Traditions." Introduction to *The Invention of Tradition*, ed. Eric Hobsbawm and Terence Ranger, 1–14. Cambridge: Cambridge Univ. Press, 1983.

Hodges, Donald C. *The Intellectual Foundations of the Nicaraguan Revolu-tion.* Austin: Univ. of Texas Press, 1986.

Hunt, Linda. "'I Could Not Figure Out What Was My Village': Gender vs. Ethnicity in Maxine Hong Kingston's *The Woman Warrior.*" *MELUS* 12, no. 3 (fall 1985): 5–12.

Hutchinson, John. *The Dynamics of Cultural Nationalism: The Gaelic Revivial and the Creation of the Irish Nation State.* London: Allen & Unwin, 1987.

Jameson, Fredric. "Third-World Literature in the Era of Multinational Capi-talism." *Social Text* 15 (1986): 65–88.

Jayal, Niraja Gopal. "Ethnic Diversity and the Nation State." *Journal of Applied Philosophy* 10, no. 2 (1993): 147–53.

Jesus, Carolina Maria de. *Child of the Dark: The Diary of Carolina Maria de Jesus.* Trans. David St. Clair. New York: Mentor, 1963.

———. *Quarto de despejo: Diário de uma favelada.* 1960. Reprint, São Paulo: Francisco Alves, 1983.

Johnston, Sue Ann. "Empowerment through Mythological Imaginings in *Woman Warrior.*" *Biography* 16, no. 2 (summer 1993): 136–46.

Kandiyoti, Deniz. "Identity and Its Discontents: Women and the Nation." *Millenium: Journal of International Studies* 20, no. 3 (1991): 429–43.

Kearney, Michael. "The Local and the Global: The Anthropology of Global-ization and Transnationalism." *Annual Review of Anthropology* 24 (1995): 547–65.

Kingston, Maxine Hong. "Cultural Mis-readings by American Reviewers." In *Asian and Western Writers in Dialogue: New Cultural Identities,* ed. Guy Amirthanayagam, 55–65. London: Macmillan, 1982.

———. *The Woman Warrior: Memoirs of a Girlhood among Ghosts.* 1976. Reprint, New York: Vintage International, 1989.

Klein, Herbert S. *Bolivia: The Evolution of a Multi-Ethnic Society.* New York: Oxford Univ. Press, 1992.

Klinghoffer, David. "Gestures of Return." Review of *Days of Obligation: An Argument with My Mexican Father,* by Richard Rodriguez. *New Criterion* 2, no. 7 (March 1993): 70–74.

Kortenaar, Neil ten. "Beyond Authenticity and Creolization: Reading Achebe Writing Culture." *PMLA* 110, no. 1 (Jan. 1995): 30–42.

Kristeva, Julia. *Nations without Nationalism.* Trans. Leon S. Roudiez. New York: Columbia Univ. Press, 1993.

Lawton, William. "The Crisis of the Nation-State: A Post-Modernist Canada?" *Acadiensis* 22, no. 1 (autumn 1992): 134–45.

Lejeune, Philippe. *On Autobiography.* Trans. Katherine M. Leary. Min-neapolis: Univ. of Minnesota Press, 1989.

Levine, Robert M. "The Cautionary Tale of Carolina Maria de Jesus." *Latin American Research Review* 29, no. 1 (1994): 55–83.

Li, David Leiwei. "The Naming of a Chinese-American 'I': Cross-Cultural Sign/ifications in *The Woman Warrior*." *Criticism* 30, no. 4 (fall 1988): 497–515.

Lovell, W. George. "Surviving Conquest: The Maya of Guatemala in Historical Perspective." *Latin American Research Review* 23, no. 2 (1988): 25–57.

Lugones, Maria. "Purity, Impurity, Separation." *Signs* 19, no. 2 (winter 1994): 458–79.

MacFarlane, S. Neil. *Superpower Rivalry and 3rd World Radicalism*. Baltimore: Johns Hopkins Univ. Press, 1985.

Menchú, Rigoberta. "The Quincentenary, a Question of Class, Not Race: An Interview with Aníbal Yáñez." *Latin American Perspectives* 19 (spring 1992): 96–100.

Miranda, Roger, and William E. Ratliff. *The Civil War in Nicaragua: Inside the Sandinistas*. New Brunswick NJ: Transaction, 1993.

Morales, Waltraud Queiser. *Bolivia: Land of Struggle*. Boulder: Westview Press, 1992.

———. "National Identity and the Ethnic Factor in Latin America: The Case of Bolivia." *Bolivian Studies* 4, no. 1 (1993): 39–58.

Muñoz, Willy O. "La conciencia de sí como arma política en *Si me permiten hablar . . . Testimonio de Domitila*." *Confluencia: Revista Hispánica de Cultura y Literatura* 2, no. 2 (spring 1987): 112–25.

Myers, Victoria. "The Significant Fictivity of Maxine Hong Kingston's *The Woman Warrior*." *Biography* 9, no. 2 (spring 1986): 112–25.

Nagel, Joane. "Constructing Ethnicity: Creating and Recreating Ethnic Identity and Culture." *Social Problems* 41, no. 1 (Feb. 1994): 152–76.

Nelson, Diane M. "Gendering the Ethnic-National Question: Rigoberta Menchú Jokes and the Out-Skirts of Fashioning Identity." *Anthropology Today* 10, no. 6 (Dec. 1994): 3–7.

Nolan, David. *The Ideology of the Sandinistas and the Nicaraguan Revolution*. Coral Gables FL: Institute of Interamerican Studies, 1984.

Nyrop, Richard F., and Thomas E. Weil. *Brazil: A Country Study*. Washington DC: Government Printing Office, 1983.

Paredes, Raymund A. "Autobiography and Ethnic Politics: Richard Rodriguez's *Hunger of Memory*." In *Multicultural Autobiography: American Lives*, ed. James Robert Payne, 280–96. Knoxville: Univ. of Tennessee Press, 1992.

Perera, Victor. *Rites: A Guatemalan Boyhood*. San Diego: Harcourt Brace Jovanovich, 1985.

————. *Unfinished Conquest: The Guatemalan Tragedy.* Berkeley: Univ. of California Press, 1993.

Pérez, Andrés. "The FSLN after the Debacle: The Struggle for the Definition of *Sandinismo.*" *Journal of Interamerican Studies and World Affairs* 34, no. 1 (spring 1992): 111–39.

Reid, Malcolm. "The Adventures of Vallières and Gagnon." *CD: Canadian Dimension* 29, no. 2 (April–May 1995): 14–18.

————. *The Shouting Signpainters: A Literary and Political Account of Quebec Revolutionary Nationalism.* Toronto: McClelland & Stewart, 1972.

Renan, Ernst. "What Is a Nation?" Trans. Martin Thom. In *Nation and Narration,* ed. Homi K. Bhabha, 8–22. London: Routledge, 1990.

Robert, Jean-Claude. *Du Canada français au Québec libre: Histoire d'un mouvement indépendantiste.* Saint-Laurent PQ: Les Éditions Flammarion, 1975.

Rodriguez, Richard. *Days of Obligation: An Argument with My Mexican Father.* New York: Penguin, 1993.

————. *Hunger of Memory: The Education of Richard Rodriguez.* New York: Bantam, 1983.

————. "The New, New World: Richard Rodriguez on Culture and Assimilation." Interview by Virginia I. Postrel and Nick Gillespie. *Reason: Free Minds and Free Markets* 26, no. 4 (Aug.–Sept. 1994): 35–41.

Rosaldo, Renato. *Culture and Truth: The Remakings of Social Analysis.* Boston: Beacon Press, 1993.

Saldaña Portillo, María Josefina. "Re-guarding Myself: Menchú's Autobiographical Renderings of the Authentic Other." *Socialist Review* 24, nos. 1–2 (1995): 85–114.

Saldívar, Ramón. "Ideologies of the Self: Chicano Autobiography." *Diacritics* 15, no. 3 (fall 1985): 25–34.

Sánchez, Rosaura. "Calculated Musings: Richard Rodríguez's Metaphysics of Difference." In *The Ethnic Canon: Histories, Institutions, and Interventions,* ed. David Palumbo-Liu, 153–73. Minneapolis: Univ. of Minnesota Press, 1995.

Sanjinés, Javier C. "From Domitila to 'Los Relocalizados': Testimony and Marginality in Bolivia." *Inti: Revista de Literatura Hispánica* 32–33 (fall 1990–spring 1991): 138–47.

Schiller, Nina Glick, Linda Basch, and Cristina Szanton Blanc. "From Immigrant to Transmigrant: Theorizing Transnational Migration." *Anthropological Quarterly* 68, no. 1 (1995): 48–63.

Schlau, Stacey. "Rigoberta Menchú, Chronicler." *NWSA Journal* 3, no. 2 (spring 1991): 262–77.

Sealey, D. Bruce, and Antoine S. Lussier. *The Métis: Canada's Forgotten People*. Winnipeg: Manitoba Métis Federation Press, 1975.

Sklodowska, Elzbieta. "Testimonio mediatizado: ¿Ventriloquia o heteroglosia? (Barnet/Montejo; Burgos/Menchú)." *Revista de crítica literaria latinoamericana* 38, no. 2 (spring 1993): 81–90.

Smith, Anthony D. "Culture, Community and Territory: The Politics of Ethnicity and Nationalism." *International Affairs* 72, no. 3 (1996): 445–58.

———. *Nations and Nationalism in a Global Era*. Cambridge MA: Polity Press, 1996.

———. "The Problem of National Identity: Ancient, Medieval and Modern?" *Ethnic and Racial Studies* 17, no. 3 (July 1994): 375–99.

Smith, Sidonie. *A Poetics of Women's Autobiography*. Bloomington: Indiana Univ. Press, 1987.

Smorkaloff, Pamela. "De las crónicas al testimonio: Sociocrítica y continuidad histórica en las letras hispanoamericanas." *Nuevo Texto Crítico* 4, no. 8 (spring 1991): 101–15.

Sollors, Werner. *Beyond Ethnicity: Consent and Descent in American Culture*. New York: Oxford Univ. Press, 1986.

Sommer, Doris. "'Not Just a Personal Story': Women's *Testimonios* and the Plural Self." In *Life/Lines: Theorizing Women's Autobiography*, ed. Bella Brodzki and Celeste Schenck, 107–30. Ithaca: Cornell Univ. Press, 1988.

———. "Rigoberta's Secrets." *Latin American Perspectives* 18, no. 3 (summer 1991): 32–50.

Staten, Henry. "Ethnic Authenticity, Class, and Autobiography: The Case of *Hunger of Memory*." *PMLA* 113 (1998): 103–16.

Vallières, Pierre. *Nègres blancs d'Amerique: Autobiographie précoce d'un "terroriste" québécois*. Montreal: Éditions Parti Pris, 1969.

———. *White Niggers of America: The Precocious Autobiography of a Quebec "Terrorist."* Trans. Joan Pinkham. New York: Monthly Review Press, 1971.

Van den Berghe, Pierre L. "The Modern State: Nation-Builder or Nation-Killer?" *International Journal of Group Tensions* 22, no. 3 (1992): 191–208.

Viezzer, Moema, ed. *"Si me permiten hablar . . . ": Testimonio de Domitila, una mujer de las mina de Bolivia*. 1977. Reprint, Mexico City: Siglo Veintiuno Editores, 1994.

Vogt, Carlos. "Trabalho, pobreza e trabalho intelectual (O *Quarto de despejo*, de Carolina Maria de Jesus)." In *Os pobres na literatura brasileira*, ed. Roberto Schwarz, 204–13. São Paulo: Editora Brasilense, 1983.

Walby, Sylvia. "Woman and Nation." *International Journal of Comparative Sociology* 33, nos. 1–2 (1992): 81–100.

Wise, R. Todd. "Native American *Testimonio*: The Shared Vision of Black Elk and Rigoberta Menchú." *Christianity and Literature* 45, no. 1 (autumn 1995): 111–27.

Wong, Sau-Ling Cynthia. "Autobiography as Guided Chinatown Tour? Maxine Hong Kingston's *The Woman Warrior* and the Chinese-American Autobiographical Controversy." In *Multicultural Autobiography: American Lives*, ed. James Robert Payne, 248–79. Knoxville: Univ. of Tennessee Press, 1992.

Woo, Deborah. "Maxine Hong Kingston: The Ethnic Writer and the Burden of Dual Authenticity." *Amerasia Journal* 16, no. 1 (1990): 173–200.

Yúdice, George. "*Testimonio* and Postmodernism." In *The Real Thing: Testimonial Discourse and Latin America*, ed. Georg Gugelberer, 42–57. Durham: Duke Univ. Press, 1996.

Index

New World Studies

New World Studies publishes interdisciplinary research that seeks to redefine the cultural map of the Americas and to propose particularly stimulating points of departure for an emerging field. Encompassing the Caribbean as well as continental North, Central, and South America, the series books examine cultural processes within the hemisphere, taking into account the economic, demographic, and historical phenomena that shape them. Given the increasing diversity and richness of the linguistic and cultural traditions in the Americas, the need for research that privileges neither the English-speaking United States nor Spanish-speaking Latin America has never been greater. The series is designed to bring the best of this new research into an identifiable forum and to channel its results to the rapidly evolving audience for cultural studies.

New World Studies

Vera M. Kutzinski
Sugar's Secrets: Race and the Erotics of Cuban Nationalism

Richard D. E. Burton and Fred Reno, editors
French and West Indian: Martinique, Guadeloupe, and French Guiana Today

A. James Arnold, editor
Monsters, Tricksters, and Sacred Cows

J. Michael Dash
The Other America: Caribbean Literature in a New World Context

Isabel Alvarez Borland
Cuban-American Literature of Exile: From Person to Persona

Belinda J. Edmondson, editor
Caribbean Romances: The Politics of Regional Representation

Steven V. Hunsaker
Autobiography and National Identity in the Americas